"As Nick's former Platoon Chief and Senior Enlisted Advisor (SEA), it is extremely gratifying to witness his success in this stage of his life as both a father, scholar, and "mentor." The professionalism and sincerity exhibited by Nick in his daily quest for the betterment of others is a testament to his warrior ethos and personal maturation from the dynamic experiences of his NSW past. I am blessed to have shared in Nick's journey."

—James S. Boa II, SOCS (SEAL) US Navy ret.

"I had the pleasure of serving with Nick during our time in SEAL training. He was and is a great man of integrity, a dedicated father and husband, and a stellar teammate. His wisdom has increased so much over our decade plus friendship, and I must say it's been a tremendous blessing to watch him grow as a leader. His ability to flawlessly pass on leadership skills acquired during his time in the SEAL Teams to corporations and professional athletes is second to none. If you want to learn how to not only be elite, but also be an elite leader, I highly recommend Elite.*"*

—Remi Adeleke, Former Navy SEAL,
author, actor and speaker

"In Nick Hays' book, Elite: High-Performance Lessons and Habits from a Former Navy SEAL, *he does a masterful job of boiling down the long-standing, well-proven secrets to success into simple, actionable steps - a masterful job of reminding us all that it's the small things that make the difference between success and failure, and that we should never, ever give up."*

—Brian P. Ward, Global Chief Executive Officer,
Trimont Real Estate Advisors

"Nick's passion for helping others succeed is only matched by his drive to share his knowledge and passion with others. Elite *is a rare glimpse into the motivation and habits Nick has used to achieve, despite everything that's stood in his path. If you're ready to learn how to take your life to the next level,* Elite *is the book for you!"*

—Bryan Black, Founder, ITS Tactical

"Against all odds, a guy who turned to humor to battle his way through some of the most challenging situations on earth. Someone everyone needs in their corner, not only in life but any professional setup that needs that extra magic. Nick Hays has the magic and it's apparent in Elite. *"Taking command of my life" in chapter 13 provides invaluable tools and made me reflect upon past adversity within my own life. I believe, and it is apparent here, that linking this to a positive outlook is what we all should strive for. Remember to take the high road, it's the road of the Elite."*

—Lysle Turner, Mount Everest Summiteer,
Harvard Alumnus, Founder of Turnvest Holdings and
the Turner Together Foundation

"This is a book for anyone. Anyone who wants to get better at anything. Whether it's personal improvement in some area of your life, improvement in your relationships, improvement in your communication with others, or improving your team, this material will help. And it applies to any environment or situation, too. Nick's training is ultra-discipline, which is crucial when others' lives are on the line. It is a mindset, a way of conducting one's life, and he shares this with us through simple language and example. Trust the content, buy the book and study it; don't just read it. If you choose not to, be content with never realizing your own full potential in life."

—Tim Anderson, Managing Director Halbert
Hargrove Global Advisors, LLC, Long Beach, CA

ELITE

ELITE

High-Performance Lessons and Habits
from a Former Navy SEAL

NICK HAYS

WILEY

Library of Congress Cataloging-in-Publication Data

Names: Hays, Nick, author.
Title: Elite : high performance lessons and habits from a former Navy SEAL /
   Nick Hays.
Description: First Edition. | Hoboken : Wiley, 2019. | Includes index. |
   Identifiers: LCCN 2018040935 (print) | LCCN 2018057709 (ebook) | ISBN
   9781119538127 (Adobe PDF) | ISBN 9781119538141 (ePub) | ISBN 9781119538097
   (hardback)
Subjects: LCSH: Leadership. | Elite (Social sciences) | BISAC: BUSINESS &
   ECONOMICS / Leadership. | BUSINESS & ECONOMICS / Motivational.
Classification: LCC HD57.7 (ebook) | LCC HD57.7 .H39133 2019 (print) | DDC
   650.1–dc23
LC record available at https://lccn.loc.gov/2018040935

Printed in the United States of America
V10009405_041619

To my parents, Kirk and Suzy Hays.
Thanks for all the hard work. I love you very much.

Contents

Introduction

Before we get started, I want you to get to know a few things about me. I am, after all, claiming to understand what makes people elite. If you were to look at my resume, you might be impressed. It would read Navy SEAL, independent contractor in a war zone, Harvard Business School student, mental skills consultant for professional sports teams, keynote speaker, active father, loving husband. Of course, the resume of an elite individual speaks only of accomplishment; the other 95% of the story is left to the imagination. My goal is to let you in on that part of the story and what I've learned along the way.

In this book, you will find structures and processes that you can easily implement in your life that will take your performance to the next level. To justify these processes, I have used some personal stories that will both demonstrate the effectiveness of the concept as well as provide some entertainment. It will be easier for you to embrace the ideas in this book if you know my history.

This introduction will give you a brief insight into the experiences that have made me who I am today. I have found that being honest about my failures and my successes equally is the best way to connect with people.

It may come as a surprise to you that I have been the underdog, and a little bit of a scrapper, all of my life. One reason for this is that I moved around every two years growing up and found myself in a perpetual state of being the "new kid in town." The result was that once I earned a spot on an athletic team or built a strong group of friends, it was time to leave and start over. Starting over was not easy. Often the moves were to different regions with their own cultures. There was always a learning curve, but this was not my biggest setback during the transition. The one factor that always leads to an uphill climb was my size. I am a short person. Like, comically short. I am nearly the perfect size to "carry a ring of power to Mt. Doom to return it to the fires from whence it came" (Tolkien, *Fellowship of the Ring*). I'm around 5 feet 5 on a good day.

My first impression with others rarely demonstrates my capability. Fortunately, I had two secret weapons that helped me meet people quickly. The first was the ability to make people laugh; people will always remember someone who made them feel lighthearted and happy. The other was athletics. I could try out for a sport and earn a spot.

Every single time I moved, there was a process. It began with an intense feeling of loss for my friends and lifestyle. Next, there was a feeling of isolation and lack of importance in the new place. Eventually, I would become comfortable in the new environment and make a group of reliable friends. Then I would experience what could be considered success at that age. Sometimes the success was with a sport, responsibility at school, or even playing guitar in a band.

Joined the Military

After I graduated high school I went to college at Ole Miss. Three of my best friends from Arizona had already joined the Navy, and two were already Navy SEALs. I had decided to go to college first but planned on joining up with them just after

I earned my degree. I thought that I had a plan, but that changed when the United States went to war.

I knew that training would take a couple of years and feared that if I didn't join the military immediately, I could miss the war entirely. Please keep in mind that none of us knew that this would become the most extended military conflict in our nation's history. I felt rushed and didn't want my friends to be over there without me.

My professional story begins with being a college dropout. I told the university that I would not be returning, and I went to the recruiter's office for passage into the Navy. Of course, when they saw me – the little guy – walk through the door, they did not take me seriously as a SEAL candidate. The guy chuckled when I told him what I wanted to do and then told me that I should be in a different job. At that time, someone who wanted to go to SEAL training had to choose a job that was called a "SEAL Source Rating." In the Navy, only a few jobs allowed the sailor to put in a package to become a Navy SEAL. They told me that, if I worked on helicopters, then I could show up to boot camp and take the screen test there.

I signed the papers and agreed to take the trip to boot camp within a month. I remember being incredibly excited when I called my friends in the Navy. One of them told me that the recruiter had lied to me about the job and that if I went into boot camp with those orders that I might never get a chance to become a SEAL. I was devastated. Not only had I been lied to, the recruiter thought that I didn't even deserve a chance to try – no doubt because of my size.

I went to the recruiter's office and told them that I knew what had happened and demanded new orders. They said no and claimed that since I had signed the contract, I was now obligated to go to boot camp and be an aircrewman my entire career. Just like any other time in my life when someone tried to outsmart me, I quickly did some research and learned as much about the subject as possible.

The recruiter hounded me over those few weeks – called me regularly, made threats, and was generally unpleasant. I'll admit that this made me feel better about what I was going to do. The day before I was on the schedule to ship out to boot camp, I showed up to the recruiter's office with a large, fresh, still-bloody tattoo on my back. I showed it to him and cited the rule that no one can ship out to boot camp within a month of getting a tattoo. I told him that my former orders would need to be rewritten and the only way he would ever see me again was if he followed the directions of my SEAL brother via phone calls. I'll never forget that look on his face – priceless.

My recruiter worked through my new set of orders with my SEAL buddies holding him accountable via phone calls, and I had the correct orders ready for me within a week. I knew exactly where I needed to be and wasn't about to let a total stranger decide for me. It was a good start, but I had a long way to go. Within a few months, I was through Navy boot camp and onto the first part of Navy SEAL training called Basic Underwater Demolition/SEAL (BUD/S) school.

Elite people know when it is time to fight for what they know is right. That fight takes its form in hard work and difficult conversations, but it is worth it in the end. I could have never accomplished my dream had I not put myself in the right position to even have the opportunity.

Setbacks

I was at BUD/S for a few months before I met a girl. She had grown up in Texas and had just finished her master's degree. She was a musical-theater actress who was doing a show on Coronado

Island, conveniently located right next to where I was in training and living at the time. It wasn't long before I asked her to marry me. I had a graduation date set and was well past Hell Week, so my odds of making it through BUD/S were good. Being a young, confident man, I decided that I could set our wedding date for the week following my graduation date. We booked a beautiful venue in San Antonio located on the famous River Walk. We sent out invitations and booked a honeymoon vacation to Cancun. Everything was rolling along, and I was feeling great.

That would soon change.

In the final weeks of our training, I had to take the last timed evolution in BUD/S. It was a two-mile ocean swim with a pass/fail time of 70 minutes. Throughout training, swimming had been my hardest test to pass. I had already failed a swim and could not afford to fail another one. The standards in BUD/S are set high and strictly maintained – and it is not a popularity contest.

A good friend at the time told me that he wanted to help me pass the swim. He brought along a dog leash to help pull me just in case we needed to make up some time. About halfway through the ocean swim, he knew that we had little hope of passing. I wanted to graduate with my class and keep my dream wedding alive so severely that I swallowed my pride and attached the leash. I fought the water like Rocky Balboa fighting Apollo Creed. I gave it everything that I had. I'll never forget crossing the finish line with my BUD/S instructor in a kayak staring at his stopwatch. "Hays, Fail," he said. It turns out that I was 10 seconds behind the time. I had tried to cheat and still failed.

Next, I would have to go before a board of instructors who would decide if I was worth keeping around in the next class. If they decided to drop me, then I would never achieve my childhood dream of becoming a Navy SEAL. Then I would have to go home and tell my fiancée that her future husband was

10 seconds too weak to provide her the dream wedding that she deserved. Never in my life had I felt like more of a failure.

I went to the board of instructors and argued my case. I told them why I wanted to be there and that I would not fail another swim if they gave me another chance. It's nice to think that my argument was compelling, but it was the authentic look of fear that I might lose my childhood dream that caught their attention. They dismissed me from the room to discuss the matter in private. So I went outside and stood at attention waiting for their decision. Tears welled in my eyes, and I felt a sickness in my gut. A few of my classmates ran past me and saw the tears running down my face, but I was so concerned with what was happening in the office that I hardly noticed.

When I went back inside, they told me that they had decided to give me another chance. I would be rolled back to the next class to go through that portion of training again. I went home to my future wife, and she told me that we would get through it together. Then I spent a month in the pool practicing my swimming technique with the best swimmers I knew. I figured that if I surrounded myself with the most elite swimmers I knew, their ability might rub off onto me. What I learned was that when you fight the water, you are creating more friction and moving slower. If you relax and get long in the water with smooth strokes, you swim faster and have the energy to spare at the end. When I rolled into the next BUD/S class, I delivered on my promise to the instructors and didn't fail a single swim. No more dog leash for me.

When I tried to cheat, I failed. When I learned from the experts, it made me a better product, and I was able to succeed. Of course, this affected my wedding date, and I had to cancel my honeymoon. There are always consequences for failure. Elite people don't let those consequences define them; they adapt to their situation, and overcome their challenges in time.

A Navy SEAL and Beyond

I graduated in BUD/S class 255 and went on to become a Navy SEAL. My military orders had me assigned to a SEAL team called SDVT-1 (SEAL Delivery Vehicle Team 1), where I would learn to pilot a miniature submersible – a small craft that the Navy uses as a deployment platform. While my friends from BUD/S were training with their platoons and eventually deploying to the Middle East, I was spending long hours diving underwater working with submarines. I will discuss this in further detail later in the book, but let's not forget that I had joined the military to join the war effort. Now, for five years, I would be stuck underwater. I feared that I would be one of the few SEALs who served during a time of war who had never been "down range" (meaning in a combat zone). I did get to do some impressive things, and the Navy awarded me with the Bronze Star, but I was unsatisfied and felt a personal goal slipping through my fingertips.

Later, I would become an instructor in San Diego for all things water. I taught combat diving, over-the-beach operations, ship boarding, and gas and oil platform assaults. Toward the end of that time, I received an invitation to try out for a new thing. The opportunity came from former teammates I had previously worked with at my SEAL team, and the "new thing" was not in the Navy. Some companies were allowing elite operators to work down range, and they were hiring on a referral basis.

I tried out for the program while I was still in the Navy and succeeded. It was quite a process, and about two-thirds of people didn't make it through the shooting and house-clearing evolutions. As I have been brutally honest about my failures, I can be frank about my achievements as well. I performed very well during the evaluations and passed everything on the first try. Perhaps I can attribute this to the fact that there was no swimming, diving, or water present.

I separated from the Navy after nine and a half years of service with an honorable discharge and a Bronze Star. Two weeks later, I was in the Middle East with a high-caliber unit doing some fantastic stuff. It's hard to express how deeply satisfying it was to be in precisely the position that I wanted to be in for so long. I found myself working with great friends, having plenty of freedom, as combat zones go, and operating at a very high level. It was intoxicating. I had finally arrived.

It was a great year. I worked multiple deployments and had a lot of fun. Getting to do the work that I had prepared so long for was extremely rewarding. The experiences I gained in the Middle East provided me with a strong sense of purpose. Unfortunately, at the end of that year, I got injured. While practicing Brazilian Jiu-Jitsu with my friends on deployment, my L5-S1 disk burst. I was flown home and needed spinal fusion surgery. With the long recovery time and the future risk of further injury, my days of working with a gun were over.

I know now that we can guess at what success might look like, but we will never really know until we are there. I learned that sometimes we do what we have to do and other times we do what we want to do. Elite people will do both to the best of their ability.

Formal Education

Don't worry, the college dropout aspect of my life was not the end of my educational story. When I had become an instructor in the SEAL teams, I had time to resume taking college classes. I attended an online option provided by the University of Maryland and finished in about a year and a half. I would teach all day and then come home and study at night. I worked through the summer semester to knock it out as quickly as

I could. I could afford to do it on a military salary because the Navy offers a tuition assistance program for active-duty service members. I had learned a thing or two about discipline through my time in the military, so my grades were top notch and I was in two honor societies. After earning my bachelor's degree, I was ready for more.

When I left the Navy to contract in the Middle East, I had applied for business school at the University of San Diego. I found that taking classes while I was home was challenging, since we had a newborn baby at the time. On deployment, my ability to learn new information, read books written by masters of business, and write papers based on what I had learned came quite easily. It wasn't until I was in my early 30s, in a war zone on the other side of the world, that I realized that I had a knack for learning. I loved business school. I needed more. As soon as I thought I'd had enough and was done with it all, I found myself plunging back in at full force. Surprisingly, I had become addicted.

Right after I was injured, I contacted multiple CEOs on LinkedIn who had businesses in San Francisco. I crafted an email detailing my history and promised that I would not ask for anything. I did not want a job or money. I was honest with them when I asked for as much knowledge as they could give me in a single sit-down meal. I told them that I would probably take notes and assured them that this was not a sales call.

What is crazy about that time in my life is that they believed me. In fact, my return rate was so high from those emails that I was able to set up three meals a day for a four-day span. I drove around the Bay Area from appointment to appointment, soaking up as much knowledge as I could. As I said earlier, I was addicted, and people were handing it out for free.

Having seen the benefit of working with extremely high-quality people in the past, with my experience as a Navy SEAL, I wondered what it would be like to go to the business school with the best reputation in the world. When you hear the word "Harvard," you can't help but associate it with the elite of the elite. Fortunately, I knew a guy who had been through Harvard Business School Executive Education. He also happened to be a close friend of mine, a SEAL who I had worked with in the past. I asked him for an introduction to the program director, and a couple of months later I started at Harvard Business School's Program for Leadership Development.

Harvard is similar to SEAL training. They aren't lying when they tell you that it is not easy and certainly not for everybody. The program stretched me mentally and culturally. Only 30% of the students in the program were from the United States, so I experienced challenging cross-cultural relations in addition to the challenging lectures. The program had a unique design: the students were responsible for trying out their ideas on everyone else while the professor facilitated the conversation. The students held the responsibility of learning new material, assessing possible strategies, and trying them out on their peers. When you are presenting your ideas to some of the brightest people on the planet, it is stressful. It was humbling, reaffirming, and extremely rewarding.

Carrier Change

Being injured was extremely challenging because I lost a large part of my identity. I had been one thing for a long time, and I saw it ripped away from me in a moment. It is when we are in those dark places of life that we have to make a choice. Will we allow ourselves to become victims or will we be warriors? I knew that I would soon be looking back at how I handled myself in those moments and I would feel one of two ways about it – embarrassed or proud. In determining what would be next for me, I thought about my "why." I knew that I needed to understand my reason for getting out of bed and working hard. Then, I needed to learn how to apply that reason to another cause in my future. It was clear that I needed a renewed sense of purpose in my life, and I needed it fast.

There was a company that had been doing workshops for college sports teams, and they had just landed their first professional sports team. They invited me to come and speak to the group about creating an elite culture. About a month after my surgery, still in a back brace, I went to work with a professional basketball team. I received some feedback that indicated I was a naturally talented speaker, so I did it again with a different team and I liked it. I realized that the rush of speaking in front of a room provided an excellent supplement for the endorphin release that you can get from jumping out of airplanes – which was nice, because my skydiving days were likely over.

I also realized that my favorite part of working overseas was helping people. My nickname as a SEAL was Nick "the heart" Hays, because of my reputation for consistently having heart-to-heart conversations with my platoon mates. I enjoyed speaking because I saw excitement and inspiration on the faces of the people I was talking to. I knew that providing them with processes that they could use in their lives would help them become truly elite, and I loved every second of it. I had my new direction.

The following year, that same company and I worked with an NFL team that was one of the worst in their division. During that year of involvement with the team, my friends and I worked with them to develop mental toughness and discipline. The team was talented, well coached, and well taught. They had a fantastic season and eventually won their way to the Super Bowl.

I realized that I was on the right track and needed to embrace this new direction at a dead sprint. It was clear that surrounding myself with elite people for my entire professional life had taught me a thing or two. My good friend Jon Gordon told me one day that because of my constant exposure to the best of the best, and because of my passion for helping people find their optimal state, sharing what I've learned was not my choice. It was my obligation. This is because elite leaders create other elite leaders. The joy and fulfillment that we get from sharing information, mentoring others, and paying it forward are what inspires the elite to stay in the game for the long haul. This realization led me to commit to sharing my ideas with the public as a speaker and a writer.

Fail Between the Lines

Let's consider my resume at the beginning of this section. At first glance, it is impressive, but now you know that between every significant high point there were vast numbers of failures. I set my goals high, got smashed back to reality multiple times, and kept going. I realized when it was time to fight for a dream. When I needed more knowledge, I committed the time it would take to become an expert. I was always aware that I could lose it all in a moment. I battled with self-doubt, fear, regret, and anger. These factors are a reality for everyone, but they will never appear on a resume. That is because our failures are not bullet points. Our successes are. It is our responsibility to make sure that we are failing between the lines. In fact, there is no other way. No one is exempt from setbacks, but not everyone will know how to learn their lessons and keep moving. Those who do are on the right path.

If you want a book written by a Navy SEAL who looks like a bulldog and talks like Batman, this book is not for you. I would never be hired to play myself in a movie. If you are looking for someone you can relate to, then you are in the right place. This book is for anyone who has been told that they can't accomplish their goals, anyone who doesn't mind admitting that they struggle with doubt or insecurity, and everyone who is open to learning the principles and practices that will allow them to get over these obstacles, and get on their way to becoming elite!

What to Expect

As you read through this book, you will notice a pattern. Every chapter will start with a fundamental principle that leads to a story. From that story, there will be some further description of the principle from an academic perspective before moving onto the practical application. I will be providing you with some ideas on how to directly apply that principle in your life to round out the chapter. I tell you this now for two reasons. One is so that you know what to expect and enter into this book with the right mindset. The second is to illustrate how this book is not intended for the critic. It is for the person who wants to be better tomorrow than they are today. To quote Theodore Roosevelt:

> It is not the critic who counts; not the man who points out how the strong man stumbles, or where the doer of deeds could have done them better. The credit belongs to the man who is actually in the arena, whose face is marred by dust and sweat and blood; who strives valiantly; who errs, who comes short again and again, because there is no effort without error and shortcoming; but who does actually strive to do the deeds; who knows great enthusiasms, the great devotions; who spends himself in a worthy cause; who at the best knows in the end the triumph of high achievement, and who at the worst, if he fails, at least fails while daring greatly, so that his place shall

never be with those cold and timid souls who neither know victory nor defeat.[1]

If you are tired of being on the sidelines criticizing others and you know that you are destined for more, this book is for you. It's time to get off the bench and into the arena.

Notes

1. Excerpt from the speech "Citizenship in a Republic," delivered at the Sorbonne in Paris, France on April 23, 1910.

Remove the Dead Weight

If you want to become elite, the most dangerous place to be in life is within your comfort zone. I know it's cozy and warm, but that doesn't make it good. Every living thing in this world is either growing or dying. In nature, nothing is static. A given organism is either improving or in decline, there is no status quo. Strength results from adversity, growth comes from effort and refinement is a product of struggle. Sure, improvement can be uncomfortable but that is okay because the pain will lead to a better product. The best way to remove dead weight is to chip away at the rough edges.

Creating a Masterpiece

I can't help but think about a large stone in the Italian country-side in the late fifteenth century. There were probably a few like it, but there was only one that would change forever. Somebody took a hammer and chisel to the stone and began cracking away pieces, which fell to the ground. The rock may not have enjoyed the process of having its edges chipped away and given a choice, may not appreciate the developmental process. For almost two years, the stone was afflicted with friction and pounding until it began to change. It had a much different look and was indeed much lighter. It was now a completely different shape, but still rough around the edges. The artist then puts away his chisel and began smoothing the stone until it held a brilliant shine.

There were multiple stones in the Italian countryside, but the great Michelangelo chose only one. He placed only one under pressure necessary to become a masterpiece, and only one is on display at Saint Peter's Basilica in Rome. Michelangelo's Pietà did not need to increase its size. It did not need more land around it. On the contrary, it needed a chisel placed on its rough edges and for the hammer to drop.

In a world geared toward increase, people are finding themselves with way too much on their plate. More food means more inches on your waistline. More expensive things mean daycare for the kids and more time at work. More square footage can result in less time at home. More digital entertainment means a clouded mind and a sedentary lifestyle. Having more of something is not necessarily good for us. In fact, elite people, teams, and companies know how to remove unnecessary things from their lives and their organizations to function more efficiently.

Learning how to be elite is about applying structures in your life that will make you stronger, smarter, and tougher today than you were yesterday. It is not going to be easy, and it may even sting a little. At times it will make you feel like a fool and also make you want to quit being so hard on yourself. You may even begin to miss your former mentality: living life as it comes, enjoying the game on TV from the couch instead of being on the field; being satisfied with your current condition with little desire for change or growth; applying the mentality it takes to become elite is hard, and that should make you smile. The fact that it is uncomfortable means that not everyone will embrace it. If this is the case, then you may indeed find yourself with the competitive edge against your rivals.

I welcome you to challenge your preconceptions and beliefs. To be open to new ideas and processes that will prove beneficial for you as an individual, and by proxy, those who are around you. I invite you to begin to see yourself as you are: an impressive piece of art. Now it's time to get the excess rock out of the way. The chisel is in place. Let the hammer drop!

Assets and Liabilities

A necessary part of becoming elite as a person, as a professional, or even at the organizational level is to remove the things that are taking more than they are giving. It's a basic concept. If I have an asset that costs more money each month, then it's not an asset at all – it is a liability. Only if an investment property I own brings in more money at the end of the month than all the expenses combined is it an asset. Apply this thinking to the way you spend your time and the people you spend that time on. When you do, you'll discover people or activities that take more away from you than they give, and you can begin to eliminate them from your life. After you've freed up the time you used to spend with these people or on these activities, you have more time to dedicate to people and pursuits that will enable you to become elite.

I know a business owner who admits to spending almost half his day in the office using social media. He's not in an industry that requires that kind of exposure and yet it's consuming his daily routine. It brings nothing but problems and costs him half a day worth of productivity. A simple press of the "Like" button invites trolls who subscribe to his feed to comment on his choice, which then requires a well-outlined defense for why he likes a video of a cat falling into uncooked scrambled eggs, despite the fact that those eggs were obviously not "free range," "grass-fed," and never had the chance to go to college. People he barely knows are giving him nothing but a headache and occupying way too much of his time. Arbitrary social media engagement is the first thing this man should eliminate. He needs to place the chisel onto the stone and let the hammer drop.

I have another friend who is a self-proclaimed foodie. If you don't know, this is someone who enjoys trying new foods and well-prepared food – a lot. I'm sure he is similar to your friend who chooses to put all his dinners on Instagram or Facebook a few times a week. He admits that nothing gives him more enjoyment than eating. Of course, he uses words like palette, tartare, and chiffonade when he talks about the food he has had. I'm not saying that this is a bad thing. We are so blessed to live in a time where food is so wonderfully crafted, but there is a catch. Too much of a good thing can kill you. His health has recently declined, and his waist size has grown as a result of poor eating habits. Were my friend to choose to eat healthy for 80% of his meals and then splurge on the remaining 20%, he would be able to keep his cholesterol in check while still enjoying his gruyère beignets.

The Backpack

The point is that we're all carrying unnecessary weight through our lives that we can eliminate. When I'm backpacking on an outdoor trail, I want everything in my backpack to have more than one use. I don't want to carry around anything I would only use once a day (other than a toothbrush … always take your toothbrush!). An example of this is my Nalgene water bottle. You might be thinking the only thing it does is hold drinking water, right? Nope. Even my water bottle has more than one use. I like to boil water in my jet boil, pour it into my Nalgene and place the container on my chest, above my base layer of clothing, and under my jacket, before falling asleep. By introducing a heat source into my sleeping bag or puffy jacket, I stay nice and warm, even when sleeping in a snow cave.

I also cut the tags off every article of clothing that I take with me because, believe it or not, ounces do add up to pounds. Apply the idea of weight in our physical world to the metaphorical weight that we all carry around, traditionally known as "baggage." How many ounces have you allowed into your life thinking that they are insignificant? Do you still keep in touch with someone from grade school even though you have both grown in different directions and have very little in common any more? Have you maintained membership in an organization simply because everyone expects you to be there? Are you in constant contact with a family member who always has a need or reason to take something but never pays his or her debts? These situations may seem harmless, but they are not. They are "time leeches" that suck away from your day's productivity and financial means. It is extra weight in your backpack that you are carrying around all the time. Why? You are not obligated to carry the load, you are choosing too.

When you allow seemingly small items to add up in your backpack, the ounces become pounds, and before you know it, you're stuck with the weight. If we eliminate the unnecessary ounces, however, we are free to run at full speed. After all, a significant part of being elite is the ability to outperform the competition.

My challenge for you is to *dump the contents of your backpack out on the ground*. Empty the pockets, the side pouches, and all the nooks and crannies. Take an inventory of the things that you have been carrying around and ask yourself why you have done so. Take a hard look at the individual ounces in your backpack and notice how those ounces quickly add up and turn into pounds. Next, consider what weight you no longer need to carry. Make sure that the items you decide to put back into your backpack either serve more than one function or that the item's single purpose is one that will lead you to your long-term goals.

Evaluate the Weight

One thing that I know for sure is that time is going to kill us all. We only have a limited amount of it, and we cannot check our balances. We never know how much we have left so choosing how to spend it is critical to our effect and presence here on earth. We will learn how to value our time more than our money, how to allocate it for max effect, and how to guard it against those who would wish to steal it. This is the responsibility of the elite individual.

I learned how to value my time because I have spent the majority of my life just giving it away. For example, when I'm working on my computer, and someone calls me on my phone, I feel bad if I don't pick up the call. The person calling doesn't know that I am working on a project. I like the person and genuinely want to talk, the problem is that I only have so much time to spend in the office, and can't afford to give it away all the time. I decided that there was no room for my cell phone in the office when I'm working. Leaving my phone in a different room allowed me to take back my time. My backpack started feeling a little bit lighter.

What are the things that you have been carrying around that are liabilities? Why have you allowed those elements to stay in your life this long? It may be time to recognize that you and only you are responsible for deciding what goes in the backpack. If you have been carrying guilt around, and feel the weight holding you down, it's time to dump out the guilt of the past to make room for the future. If you have been carrying around insecurity that has made it hard to walk, let alone run, then it's time to dump the insecurity on the ground so that you can embrace the confidence that comes with taking charge of the weight you are willing to carry. If there are people in your life that don't believe in you or want what's best for you, bullies, negative coworkers, or people who never have a positive thing to say about anybody, consider removing them from your backpack and making room for people who will care about you, share in your successes, and brighten your day.

Finally, if you have been clinging to certain beliefs, practices, or habits, and they are no longer working for you, it's time to dump those outdated ideas on the ground. Elite people are lifelong learners. They recognize that they will never have it all figured out, so they take on new ideas and try them out. Make room in your backpack by being open-minded as you approach this book. I will be sharing principles with you that I have observed from other Navy SEALs, Harvard students, and professional sports teams. I will also be sharing from my personal experience – the things that worked for me and why. Now that there is room in your backpack let's start filling it with the high-performance lessons and habits of the elite!

Becoming Elite!

1. Make peace with the fact that you need to remove the rough edges and excess weight from your life and commit to taking action.
2. Identify the unnecessary weight that you have allowed in your backpack, realize that you are not obligated to carry it, and dump it out on the ground.
3. Value your time, value your experiences, recognize when others are taking more than they are giving and when it is time to cut loose the extra weight.
4. Refuse to be bullied by negativity or undue obligation.

CHAPTER

2

No More Excuses

I was watching a recent episode of *Shark Tank* when I heard something that struck a nerve. It was more than mere conviction. It was like catching a punch straight to the face. Occasionally, I will listen to someone addressing an audience, yet I feel that he or she is speaking directly to me. The sharks saw something in the man's pitch, and they would have seen it in myself had I been there. They ultimately chose not to partner with the man for one reason: He was a perfectionist.

This contestant had spent almost five years in research and development and would have been a fast mover in this market. I wanted to buy the product myself while watching his pitch. The sharks must have seen the value but decided not to partner with him because he was bogged down by the idea that everything had to be in its optimal, perfect, and omniscient state before going to market. Driving revenue was less important to this man than the brilliant shine on his product.

As I said, it hit a nerve. I have been guilty of this for different reasons at nearly every point in my life. Hearing these successful venture capitalists describe perfectionism as a significant character flaw dramatically impacted my life. I started peeling back the onion of my insecurities and didn't like what I saw. It dawned on me that I was using my perfectionist trait as an excuse. I always needed more time, more quality control, more input. But all I'd been getting was less: less output, less involvement, and less momentum. Sitting in my living room with only the blue light from the TV for illumination, I realized something essential. As long as I was a perfectionist, I would never be elite. Perfectionism was a convenient excuse for not writing, speaking, and sharing my ideas with others. My quest for perfect had left me crippled with excuses.

Fall from Perfect

It's difficult to be vulnerable as a writer, but it's also impossible to write without leaving yourself vulnerable. I had found myself in a rare and precarious position. I had recently separated from the Navy where I served as a SEAL for the better part of a decade. I had also spent time deployed while attending business school. Additionally, when I was in the United States, I was always on the move in the family RV (28,000 miles in three years, to be exact). I never had the desire to write about my work on the operational level, but I've traveled so much and met so many amazing people that I found myself with quite a bit to say about life, finding happiness through excitement, and the pursuit of balance, both mentally and physiologically. I have had the fortune to meet and work with the highest quality of professionals from all over the world. My life has exposed me to so many worldviews, socioeconomic conditions, and personality types that I'm inspired to share what I've learned with others.

Despite having inspiration, a message that people needed, and a word processor, I was unable to get going. In fact, the act of sharpening my pencil had become more important than putting that pencil to paper. I had all the excuses that I needed contained inside the justifiable, shiny box of perfectionism. The purpose of my excuse: to compensate for all my insecurities, and my fear of failure.

If you find yourself with an excuse preventing you from taking action, ask yourself if that excuse is hurting your productivity. If your excuse is that you don't want others to see your work until it is perfect, then get used to disappointment. I hate to break it to you but you are not capable of producing a perfect work, nor should you want to. It is our imperfections that provide character to our work. Learn to embrace those imperfections and your work will likely go from good to great. After all, it's not about being perfect. It's about being elite.

Take Action

The opposite end of the spectrum of perfectionism is laziness. Many people make excuses based on their being too tired, too weak, and unmotivated to take action. Where the perfectionist was making excuses from a position of high energy and stress, the person who struggles with laziness is coming from a position of low energy, low stress, and even boredom – two very different people with very different lifestyles who have the same problem of making excuses.

If you have ever found yourself thinking that you are too tired or too busy to get to the gym, then you will never become physically capable and healthy unless you identify those excuses as a negative function and choose to take action. Those thoughts are heavy to carry around in your backpack, and your life will be better off without them. Sure, you may not be able to lift the same amount of weight as you used to as a young man, but that is not a good excuse to avoid the gym. You don't need excuses. You need more repetitions and the subsequent experience. The more you work out, the stronger you will become. The same is true for your mind. If you identify your excuses as the problem, you can begin to train your mind to look past those excuses and to see the need for action.

Find Your Optimal Performance

When you're driving on the road, if you go too far to the right, you will hit a ditch. Remember that the same is true for veering off too far to the left. There are pitfalls on both extremes of the road. Good advice for the person veering to the left would be to come back to the right. If that person listened to advice that he or she should continue going left, that advice would have a negative impact. The same advice will not work for everyone because we are all coming from different places. We have a responsibility to make sure the information that we accept and the processes that we place in our lives will work for us. What works for someone else may not necessarily work for you. Before you can implement the tools of the elite into your life, you must first learn where you currently are, then identify where you want to be. Find the root of your excuses.

Inverted U and Stress Control

Here's an example: We all live on a dial from 1 to 10. For this analogy, the dial represents our intensity level. One is the most relaxed a person can be, whereas 10 is the most fired up. As the 1 gets ready for a high-pressure situation, he may benefit from listening to rock music beforehand to get from a 1 on the dial to a 4. Conversely, the person who is at a 10 will need to listen to classical music to slow his heart rate down to a 6. Your default state will ultimately determine what direction you should go to find the center.

The inverted U was created by Robert Yerkes and John Dodson in the early 1900s. It has stood the test of time because it does a great job of showing the connection between the pressure a person is under and his or her performance. As you can see from Figure 2.1, the 1 on the dial mentioned earlier represents low pressure, stress, or boredom. The 10 is high stress, high pressure, and anxiety. The arch represented by the line demonstrates the level of our ability to perform. Our best performance will take place when our stress levels are toward the middle of the road. Too much stress will inhibit your performance, as will too little. Two people located on opposite ends of the dial will require two different solutions.

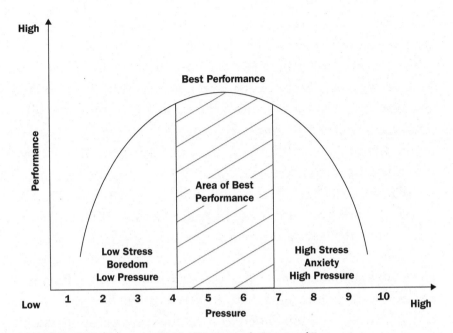

FIGURE 2.1 Inverted U, "Arousal Control"

Let's relate this to the excuses that we make. If you have to give a presentation at work and are nervous about it, you may find yourself closer to the 10 spot, experiencing high stress, rapid breathing, and anxiety. Your excuses will reflect this. You will tell yourself that someone else is better suited to give the presentation. You will say to yourself that you don't need the stress and would be better off without it. The excuse could come in many forms, but your goal in making an excuse will be to eliminate the stress.

Here's the rub. You're right to think the stress should be mitigated, but giving up on the presentation is not your solution. What you need are repetitions. Just like working out at the gym, the more you work out, the stronger you become. In this case, the more you deliver presentations, the less stress you will feel when presenting over time. Do not lose an excellent opportunity to demonstrate your talent and ability because of an excuse born of anxiety.

Now, let's talk about the low-pressure side of the model – the low-stress, boredom side of the house. Have you ever made a New Year's resolution only to give up on it before the end of January? Was the resolution based on being physically fit, active, and healthy? If this is the case, congratulations, you're normal. We have all allowed our excuses to get the better of us at some point, myself included. If you find yourself too tired, too busy, too (insert weakness here) then you may be living as a 1 or 2 on the dial. Your excuses are coming from that position.

There are ways of moving from a 2 on the dial to a 5, none of them involve laying down and watching TV. If you are able to recognize where the excuse is coming from, then you can make an adjustment. Don't think. Get your shoes on and go for a leisure walk. Before you know, it your body will be more awake and you will be more inclined to continue walking and possibly even pick up the pace. Or, you can sleep in your gym clothes. Eliminate the chance of your brain's making excuses as I have. Giving yourself less time to think about the activity you want to do will benefit you.

Find Peace in Admitting Your Fear

Most perfectionists make excuses because they are afraid that their work will not live up to other people's – or their own – expectations. People who struggle with boredom and laziness make excuses based on the amount of work in front of them and rationalize their lack of action because they don't feel like they will stick with it. Both are afraid of failure. Fear is not a bad thing. It's one of the reasons we have survived as a species. Here is an example: The caveman knew that sleeping in a fortified position was necessary because he was appropriately afraid of predators. This emotion kept our early ancestors alive.

They knew they would be hunted after dark and embraced their very rational fear. Their fear was rooted in awareness, knowledge of their environment, and the will to survive. It is healthy.

Of course, too much of one thing always has a negative impact. If the caveman were too afraid to leave the cave, then he would starve to death within a month. In this case, an absence of fear would lead to the caveman's death, as would too much fear. The point is that fear can be beneficial and is acceptable, but don't use it as an excuse not to take action when action is required.

The Potential of Failure Is Not an Excuse

Fear of failure is something that everyone has felt from time to time because it is a normal response to the unknown. Whether it was asking a girl to dance in junior high or talking to your boss about a promotion as an adult, failure is scary. When you read my story in the prologue, did the amount of failure in the story strike you? As you know, my entire journey was fraught with multiple small failures. What those situations provided me was valuable experience. If we never fail, then we will never gain the knowledge that we need to succeed. And if we never try, we will never have the opportunity to fail. Yes, failure is an opportunity, not an excuse. Elite people will learn something every time they fail and become a better product as a result. Your failure is temporary. If you are wrong today, you will have another opportunity tomorrow. Wrong is not forever. Elite people do not use fear of failure as an excuse. They know that they will fail along the way and the embrace the opportunity to gain valuable experience.

If you can separate your value and self-worth from your ability to produce a perfect product or never fail, then you will no longer need excuses. You will find yourself embracing the harder problems because of the joy of discovering a solution. You will start having more fun because the cloud of judgment is no longer on your shoulders. When you begin to have fun, your work will soar to new levels because you will work harder, spend more time in thought, and start to enjoy the process. You will apply the lessons that you have gained from experience, and future projects will have fewer setbacks.

Becoming Elite!

1. When you catch yourself making excuses, identify your location on the "inverted U." Do what it takes to find your optimal performance zone.
2. Consider what opportunities you have allowed to slip through your hands due to unproductive excuses.
3. Embrace your fear. Fortify the areas in which the fear is justified so that you can rest easy.
4. Start looking for ways to gain experience and stop listening to excuses.

3

Take Control of Your Thoughts

Have you ever felt like you are walking a tightrope between insecurity and arrogance? One day you wake up feeling on top of the world like nothing can stand in your way. If you quit your job, you'd have it replaced by the end of the day. If you wanted to be the president of the United States, you could accomplish it with a single tweet.

Then the next day, you wake up and wonder how you've been able to Forrest Gump your way this far through life. Undoubtedly, it was some lucky mistake, and the bottom is about to drop out. You start thinking that you aren't good enough for anything that you have and you don't deserve the love of anyone who would give it.

If this daily pendulum shift description sounds familiar, guess what, you're not alone. Everyone, even the elite people of any industry struggle with controlling their thoughts. We're such fickle beings and our mental state shifts like a blade of grass blown by the wind. One minute, we view ourselves with too much esteem and the next with too little. Finding that balance is one of the most challenging things a person can do. In this chapter, we will apply what we learned from the inverted U of stress control to our thought lives. Some thoughts are beneficial, and some are harmful to our quality of life as well as our ability to perform. Being able to control those thoughts will make a dramatic difference in your life, but first, you need to be able to identify what part of the dial you are currently on.

The Confidence Dial

In Chapter 2, we looked at the inverted U as a method of identifying the origins of our excuses. Now imagine that the left side represents our mental state when we're depressed, down on ourselves, and functioning with low self-esteem (see Figure 3.1). The right side represents when we're overconfident, blissfully ignorant, and our egos are running amuck.

If you wake up from a bad dream where someone you trust disappointed you, or your boss was telling you how worthless you are, then you might find yourself immediately on the low end of the dial, closer to the 1.

The same is true for the person who gets a big bonus with a promotion and is snapping their fingers singing Frank Sinatra's "I've Got the World On a String" on his way out of the office

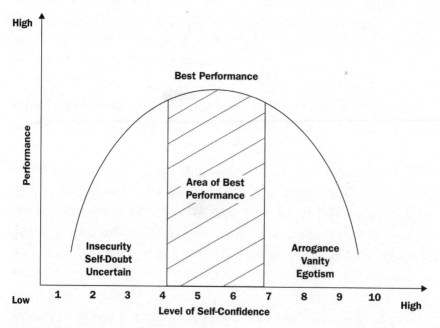

FIGURE 3.1   Inverted U, Part 2

and to a bar with an attractive coworker, instead of going home to his or her family. This person is currently closer to the 10 on the dial. Unfortunately, his or her overconfidence could lead to serious problems. Simply knowing where you exist on that dial currently will give you the edge moving forward because you will know what direction to travel.

Insecurity

Believe me, I've been down in the dumps. Remember when I was injured while deployed in the Middle East and had to get spinal fusion surgery? I knew that I'd need to find a new career and endure a considerable amount of pain through recovery. During that year, I experienced some significant lows. It was challenging financially, and I gained weight from having to lie down all the time. I'd never felt such a strange brew of emotions before. The classic demon from the old cartoons showed up on my shoulder and started whispering harsh words in my mind. "You're the shell of a man that you once were," the negative demon would say.

Adding to my stress was the fact that my wife was pregnant with our third child, and babies aren't cheap. Although we'd been living in our RV and traveling the country, with the pregnancy and new baby coming, we had to get into a home. I couldn't afford it, and for some time I had no idea what to do.

Around this time, a good friend of mine offered me an opportunity to come live in his company apartment in exchange for working as a project manager for his specialty construction company. A great thing for my family – "charity case," the demon whispered – although it meant that I'd be working through the painful recovery process. "Weakling." At least I would be off the couch – "still fat."

We got settled in, and I enjoyed working with my friend. It was a great office environment, and we took regular breaks to throw the football, which is my favorite thing to do. My wife had a decent pregnancy, and in the spring, we were blessed with a beautiful baby girl.

While this was all great, I didn't feel well at all. I was lethargic and tired all the time. I knew it was bigger than my surgery recovery, so I went to the doctor. I had a CBC blood test, and the results were less than encouraging. My blood platelet level was 969, with the usual range being less than 200.

I remember seeing my newborn baby's face in my mind's eye as the doctor told me that I might have leukemia. The next couple of months were a nightmare. I had once been an elite individual, but now my life had gone downhill so quickly that I was unprepared for what I was experiencing and the demon bellowed with laughter. Despite the bad news, I was committed to staying positive and pushing forward.

That's when things began to change. I was at a golf tournament helping a brother of mine from the SEAL teams with his nonprofit when I met another SEAL who was helping get veterans to the appropriate treatment programs for their medical recovery. He told me I didn't look so great and asked me if I could use some help. He offered to send me to a clinic in Florida where they take athletes after severe injuries and get them back on the field. They had a tactical athlete program as well, and he said I was the perfect candidate. It gave me something that had been absent from my life for some time – namely, hope. I'm not sure why, but the demon didn't show up on that day. I could almost hear something click as I moved from a 1 to a 2 on the dial.

Two months after hearing the bad news from the doctor, I had a bone marrow biopsy, and it showed that I did not have leukemia. Instead, it was my body reacting negatively to major surgery. It was a condition to be mindful of moving forward, but not life-threatening. A couple of months later, I was at the clinic in Florida, and for the first time in a year, I was able to touch my toes. Another click had me feeling much more confident and capable as I moved from a 2 to a 3 on the dial.

Over the next year or so, the demon still showed up from time to time, but his voice is beginning to carry a little less weight in regards to my physical ability and mental clarity. I had been climbing back up the dial toward my zone of optimal performance.

Knowing where we are on the dial is the perfect place to start, but it's not the whole story. Next, we need to identify how to travel in the direction that will take us away from polarity and back to our zone of optimal performance. If you can proactively control your thoughts, then you will lead a more productive, freedom-filled, happy life.

Here are some methods you can use to dial it up to center when you have identified the negative tipping point.

Replace Negative Thoughts with Positive Thoughts

You're not the voices in your head; they're just trying to have a say. Your mind is kind of like social media: know when to "like" and when to hit the block button. Removing the demon from your head will allow you to control your mind and will let you keep from spiraling down the rabbit hole of self-doubt and nega-tivity. Of course, often when we tell the demon to shut up, it only makes us focus on what he is saying. Not good enough. The strategy is not only to remove the negative demon, but instead replace him with positivity.

Thought replacement is a mental toughness tactic that I have used a lot over the course of my life. When someone I respected told me that I would never become a Navy SEAL, I would imag-ine the day that I would tell him or her I had been successful, and I could imagine how rewarding that would feel. I even had to use thought replacement while writing this book. When other veterans say that I should never write a book because veterans should be "silent professionals," I think about how many people I can help by sharing my perspective. Instead of allowing that kind of negativity into my mind, I embrace my ability to bring positive insight into other people's lives. I'll never be silent, but I can indeed be a positive professional who is in control of his mind.

Replacing negative thoughts with positive ones is a skill set that you must practice on your journey to becoming elite. It is a technique called self-talk. It is a way to be deliberate about what is replacing your negative thoughts. For example, if you hear the negative demon growl, "You're an idiot" then tell yourself, "I'm learning so much every day, I can't wait to see where I'll be in a year." Practice replacing, "you're going to fail" with, "win or lose, this will be fun, and I'll learn a lot." "You're ugly," turns into "I'm intelligent, healthy, and I feel great. What is sexier than that?"

Self-talk is not always smooth and requires practice. The good news is that if you commit to it, your positive thoughts will start to become second nature. If you agree to do that work and practice the skill, you will begin to enjoy your own company. You will no longer fear your imagination because it has been trained to see the endless amounts of opportunities that you have available. You can begin to explore a future that you are actively creating. You will know that the practice is paying off when people start asking you to tell them about the source of your joy. Be sure to pay it forward whenever you can by sharing your strategy.

Put Things into Perspective

Next, try to pull yourself out of your limited viewpoint and look down at your situation from a bird's eye view. Looking back at your problems from a different perspective will allow you to see things that you did not see before.

When I am about to speak to a large crowd, I get a little nervous. The accomplished comedian Jerry Seinfeld told a joke in his comedy special, *Live on Broadway* that addressed the nerves associated with public speaking. He said, "The number one fear in America is public speaking. Number two is death. This means that at any given funeral, the average American would rather be in the casket than performing the funeral."

Even though I've been speaking publicly for a while now, I care about my craft so much that I get a little bit nervous. When this happens, I try to add some perspective by reminding myself of the fact that no one will even remember this in five years. In fact, we're all going to die someday. I could trip and fall off the stage, tearing my pants and leaving me in tears as I run out of the room at top speed. In 60 years, no one will even be alive to remember. There is some perspective.

Enjoy the people who love you, play with your kids, call your friends and tell them how much they mean to you. Have sex with your wife – I mean, hug your wife. Find your higher power and hold on tight. When we realize that we will all fade to ash, our current problems seem so small. We can't take anything with us when we are gone, not even our problems. It is our responsibility to not live in our minds, but to break free, use our eyes, and live presently in the moment. When you play with your kids, try not to think about work problems or money problems. Instead, look at the way your kids smile and laugh. Enjoy them because they will eventually outgrow times like these and you will only have the memories that you're making in that fleeting moment. Someday, this will all end, so live in the moment, create memories, and accept your responsibility to enjoy the ride.

Thinking about this life as temporary causes us to live like there is no tomorrow. A little bit of perspective shows me that I should be much more afraid of not speaking in front of the group that I am from actually speaking. I don't know how much time I have so I need to fill it with the things that matter. If you have been stuck in a dead-end job and are afraid of making a change, try writing down your fears on paper. Next, put those fears into perspective. Is getting your resume out there really that scary? What is the worst that could happen? The ability to put your problems into perspective will help you make a click on the dial back into the direction of optimal performance.

Levity

Next, learn to use humor to your advantage. A little bit of levity goes a long way. I know from experience I can stare the demon in the face and laugh. It's hard to illustrate how powerful a dynamic this is. The harder things get, the funnier they can become. I learned this at BUD/S (SEAL training). The colder and the wetter the class is, the better the jokes are. I have seen this time and time again. A person is most powerful when they can laugh, even in the darkest of places.

I'll never forget a summer morning, when I was deployed to a combat zone, overseas working in another dangerous environment I had come to know too well. We were all woken up by the sound of an explosion, which was evidently the sound of a vehicle-borne improvised explosive device (VBIED). Small arms fire immediately followed the explosion. I was sleeping with my body armor and weapon ready, but I wanted to get to the roof of the building and wasn't comfortable with that idea unless I could grab a helmet. I ran into a small room that we had turned into storage to grab a helmet and saw three of my friends who had the same thought.

The look on everyone's face was of surprise and even a little bit of fear. Being startled awake by an ambush had shaken everyone up, at least better than a cup of coffee would have. For some reason, I was compelled to quote the movie *Braveheart* as I said in my best Scottish accent, "That'll wake you up in the morning, boys." I'll admit, the joke was well placed and hit the spot. We all started laughing, grabbed our helmets and went on with what would become a long day; I'll share more of that story later. Add a little bit of levity in a tough moment helped us all get our heads back in the game.

Elite people are good at rising to the occasion. Levity is a way of cutting a problem down to size and recognizing that it is not too big for you to handle. When you can laugh at something, it has no power over you. Please do not confuse this with mockery, however. Mockery is rooted in ridicule, contempt, and scorn. Levity is rooted in liveliness, good humor, and cheerfulness. Elite people know that you must first respect the problem before you can rise to the occasion. Levity is one tool that you can use to raise your position on the dial from a 2 to a 5 within moments.

Make Big Things Small

Finally, take everything one step at a time. We've all heard the saying, "How do you eat an elephant? One bite at a time." You have to make the more intimidating things in your life more manageable by setting smaller, more attainable benchmarks. In SEAL training, we learned this lesson from our instructors. They taught us this lesson in a classroom and then provided us multiple opportunities to practice. Hell Week in particular drove this point home. In one week we ran over 200 miles, were cold, wet, and miserable consistently and only slept for two hours total. The people who thought about the end of the week on Monday did not get through the rest of the day. The weight of the total picture was too much to bear. It was too long, too hard, and too . . . the demon growls with an evil smile.

The trick was to make such a big, insurmountable problem smaller and more attainable. I knew that the instructors were going to feed us meals like clockwork. They had to operate within the rules after all. Instead of thinking about the end of the week, I could think about the hot meal that was coming in a couple of hours. The instructors could hurt me for a while but eventually, that hot meal was coming, and no one could take that away from me. "Get to the hot meal, and nothing else matters," I would say to myself. Whatever you're facing, cut it into pieces that are easier to digest mentally. Get to the next hot meal.

When getting to the meal seemed like too much, then I would think about different muscle groups in the body. When the instructors had us lifting massive telephone pole like logs over our heads, it made our shoulders burn like fire. I would tell myself that they are almost done with shoulders and will have to focus on a different muscle group soon. After a shoulder exercise, they would often move to a workout that would put stress on the legs instead. I would use self-talk to tell myself, "just get to legs. Then my shoulders will rest." Even when getting to the next meal seemed overwhelming, I was able to break it down into something even smaller like what muscle group was coming next.

You can apply this way of thinking to your goals. If you want to become a CEO of a company someday, developing a strategy to get there can be intimidating and even discouraging. It is like saying that you want to bench press 300 pounds. If you were to try and lift 300 pounds today, your body might not be able to withstand the weight if you have not prepared. It's much better to say that you want to be able to bench press 150 pounds by the end of the month (or whatever is manageable for you), 200 pounds within six months, and 300 pounds in a year. I know that

I want to get to 300 pounds in the back of my mind, but I know what I have to do today to get to this month's goal. Now that is an encouraging thought process.

If becoming a chief operations officer is the goal of your professional life, then don't be discouraged about how far you have to go. Rather, you need to ask what a COO needs to know to do his or her job well. The answer may be more knowledge of the company and more experience in operations. Next, decide how you can accomplish this one step at a time. If you set a goal of becoming a project manager, then you will learn valuable lessons. These lessons will make you a better product and lead you closer to your long-term dream. Focus less on where you want to be long term and think more about what you can do today. Elite people get to where they want to be by setting smaller, more attainable goals, which make the big things seem small.

Arrogance

Although the low end of the dial can be terrible, the high end can be equally perilous. It causes us to be reckless and reliant on getting lucky. The Greeks call it hubris, the belief that your greatest strength will eventually be your undoing. Remember when Thetis, Achilles's mother, dipped her half-god son into the river Styx? It was said to have great power to protect him.

Unfortunately, she was holding him by the ankle, which left that small area as the only chink in his armor. Achilles believed he was next to immortal and forgot his weakness until an arrow from the bow of a much lesser man struck him in his heel. This story is a cautionary tale for the high end of the scale. When we forget our weaknesses and shortcomings entirely, we're left vulnerable.

I'll never forget the first few weeks of my Harvard Business School experience. I had already completed my master's degree and was very confident in my academic ability. I mean that I was "Achilles" confident. I was taking an accounting class at the time and had enjoyed the assignments. I hadn't had much experience in accounting at all so the exposure was fun and the learning curve was steep. I went into my first exam knowing that I had studied, worked hard, and deserved to be there. You can imagine my dismay when I got my first exam back and saw that I had earned a D. Welcome to Harvard, and back to earth. My overconfidence had taken the place of reality. I learned that I was operating too much on the high end and needed to come back to center. My confidence had, in fact, turned to arrogance.

Be Confident, Not Arrogant

I can look back at my life and see how every time I got a little over confident, the universe had a way of smacking me back down to size. Remember when I asked my wife to marry me in BUD/S? We planned our wedding to take place only a week after I'd graduated from training. When I failed that two-mile ocean swim by 10 seconds and got rolled back into another class, missing the graduation date that my wedding and honeymoon was dependent on, I realized that I had been arrogant, not confident. My consequence was that instead of the stress-free wedding of our dreams, I had to fly out after training ended on a Friday afternoon, get married in Texas and fly back through the night; only to meet the members of class 255 for land navigation in the mountains of Southern California. What a honeymoon it was!

There's a fine line between confidence and arrogance. We all want to be confident in everything we do, and we should want that. However, when that confidence goes too far, we find ourselves too arrogant to know we're staring hubris in the eyes.

Our zone of optimal performance on the Inverted U is confidence. When we find ourselves sitting at an eight on the dial, that confidence turns to arrogance. Confidence is knowing that you're up to the task. Arrogance is thinking that you're above it. For this reason, elite athletes train extremely hard. Athletes do not feel like they are above the training because they know that the more practice they get, the more likely they are to succeed. When they wake up in the morning with the thought, " I should sleep in, I'm too talented for this," they know how to replace that thought with, " If I am going to be the best, I will need to work the hardest. Everyone is talented in the league, but champions go the extra mile."

If you're killing it at work and are finally getting the recognition you deserve, but start thinking you're too important to take out the trash at the office, be careful. Your scale is tipping.

Remember, arrogance is the high end of the scale and confidence is the balance. You can achieve confidence through proper training, practicing the mental techniques in this chapter, and being aware of your strengths and weaknesses. Arrogance comes when you deny those things, thinking that you're somehow above the rules of this world.

Humility

I'll be honest with you. I was worried that using the word *elite* for this book would make some of you think of narcissism, arrogance, and egotism. I assure you that this is not the case at all. Performing at a high level is not an excuse to be an ass. In fact, you will find the cockier a person is, the less experience they probably have. When we raise the quality of our performance, we find ourselves with more opportunities to perform. With more opportunity comes more exposure. The more exposure gained, the easier it becomes to stay humble.

I'm not cocky because I went to Harvard. The experience humbled me because I've seen what smart looks like. I've seen the competency level of a specialized professional in their particular field compared to someone who is getting their first look at that field. I've sat in a group of eight people who all have very different methods of preparing for a lecture. Should I have told them that they were wrong because they were not doing it my way? By no means! They were exceptional people, and although I would offer my point of view when appropriate, I had so much to learn from the people in that room.

You will never be elite until you learn to humble yourself. Arrogance and narcissism will lead you down a path of misery and failure. Consider this: I have never been in a room where everyone in that room didn't know more about something than me. Regardless of education or accomplishment, every person in this world has something to teach me. Arrogance is the enemy of learning and the sharing of knowledge. Humility is the key to seeing the value in other people, learning as much as possible, and being able to perform at an elite level. When you have arrogant thoughts, replace them with thoughts of humility and respect.

I encourage you to identify on what end of the dial you spend most of your time. Make an effort to use these methods to train your mind to always move toward your zone of optimal performance. If you are insecure, then use thought replacement, perspective, and levity to move from insecure to confident. If you realize that you've allowed arrogance to cloud your vision, consider embracing humility – recognizing that everyone has something to teach – and open-minded conversation to bring you back to center. Finding your confidence is key to becoming elite.

Becoming Elite!

1. Take a hard look at your positions on the confidence scale. If you are insecure or arrogant, acknowledge it and commit to change.
2. When the negative demon growls, have a response ready to silence it and replace it with realistically positive truth.
3. Practice these techniques as much as possible. Incorporate them into your daily life to make positive, humble thoughts a habit.
4. Be up to the task, not above it. Arrogance will undermine you so get rid of it.
5. Take out the trash at work with a smile, regardless of your job title.

CHAPTER
4

Be Mentally Tough

The idea of accomplishing a seemingly insurmountable goal like Hell Week by setting smaller, more attainable goals like getting to your next meal is not an original idea. When I got to BUD/S, my class had an instructor assigned to us who had the responsibility of mentoring us through the program. He shared advice on different mental tricks, and that was one that he taught us. I remember that idea resonating with me because it was a tool that I had used many times before. It validated a process that I had placed in my life and gave me a reason to keep making big things small by cutting them down into smaller, easier to attain goals. This story is about one of the first times that I learned to take control of my thoughts to accomplish a challenging goal. When we can put our minds to work for us, we become mentally tough.

Climbing High

I grew up outdoors and always had an intense love for the mountains. I spent my entire life before high school living in mountainous regions in the western states. My parents taught me how to make fire, fish, camp, and hike from a young age and I am thankful for it, although they may have regretted it a little as I grew into a teenager.

I have always pushed a little harder than those around me and have been in constant search for my limits. It was when I lived in Tucson, Arizona, when I met a few other guys who were in search of their limits as well. We might have seemed different or counterculture to our classmates, but we had a great deal in common with each other. It was one of the tightest groups of friends that I have ever had. We were on the same wrestling team, we enjoyed working out, and we were rarely indoors. In fact, when we were together the ideas would flow, and excitement would build as we found ways to get in over our heads.

One time, we decided that crossing the most prominent mountain in the area would be a fun adventure. The mountain is called Mount Lemmon, and it is no joke. At the base, the elevation is 2,700 feet. The summit is over 9,000 feet. That is quite an elevation gain for a few junior high kids, especially if you consider that the trail started on the north side of the mountain and ended on the south side. Our chosen path was a 45-mile trek that went straight up and then straight down again. Needless to say, we couldn't wait to get up there.

Humble Beginnings

Now, as a well-trained Navy SEAL, I look back at what we would carry in our backpacks on these overland adventures, and it makes me laugh. Instead of water bladders, we bought plastic gallons of water. Instead of freeze-dried Mountain House meals and a Jetboil we had cans of spaghetti and beans. It was an archaic, poor man's loadout in every way, but my friend Dan was always kind enough to supply the group with red Twizzlers whenever we would venture into the wilds. I tell you this because of the weight that it added to the packs. We carried everything in its heaviest form because we didn't know any other way. Elite we were not.

On the morning of my first day, my mom dropped us off at the trailhead for Romero Pools. I'm not sure if my mom thought that dropping off five kids in mountain lion country for half a week with no communication methods was a good idea, if she just really trusted us, or if she knew that she would never be able to convince us that it was a bad idea. Either way, I was lucky to have a mom that allowed me to be a young man.

When we dismounted the vehicle, said our goodbyes to the only adult, and put on our backpacks, there was a sense of excitement that is hard to describe. Sure, I was a little scared of what could happen. I could get snakebite, heat exhaustion, or fall of a cliff. I put those thoughts out of my mind and looked up at the beautiful mountain that loomed above with awe and anticipation. The Sonoran Desert is a lovely site. For a desert, it is oddly green. The Palo Verde trees have green bark, so they don't need leaves to brighten the deserts appearance. The Jumping Cholla cactus has thousands of white spikes sticking out in every direction. These spines shine brightly in the sun and make the Cholla look like they are glowing with a white flame. The most breathtaking plant that I have ever seen lives in that area as well – the saguaro cactus. It is the cactus featured in the old Road Runner cartoons that sticks up out of the ground and has arms coming out of it like a hat rack. Of course in real life they are majestic.

A Long Way to Go

A giant saguaro was standing tall right next to the trailhead. It was healthy and green, and with the mountain behind it, the scale of it all was intimidating. It takes close to 100 years for this cactus to grow one arm, and doesn't reach its full height of 50 feet until it is 150 years old. At 50 feet tall it loomed above me and yet I couldn't see any up on the mountain. I knew they were there, but I couldn't even see them. It was going to be a long hike.

The first leg of the hike was to Romero Falls, which was an oasis that sat on the mountainside. Locals hiked up to it to enjoy a break from the hardcore Arizona heat. We got there relatively early in the afternoon but had planned to spend the night because it is the perfect place to camp. We had been to this spot in the past and had jumped off of every cliff available. There is a short jump, about 25 feet or so, in a pond that functions as an oasis from the southern Arizona heat. The locals come to the pools to cool off and relax. Just downstream is a smaller pool with a much bigger cliff to jump. It is around 55 feet, depending on the depth of the water, and the landing area is a small target. Jumping off that cliff takes some nerve. It was enough of a fall to send your stomach into the back of your throat, and because you had to clear an ocotillo cactus and hit a small landing zone, that first step was a little harder than usual. Romero Pools was where I first fell in love with being up high and jumping off things. Later I would start jumping out of airplanes and helicopters without hesitation, but it all started at Romero Pools jumping off cliffs.

The Ascent

After a relaxing evening, we woke up, loaded our packs and took off up the mountain. By midday, the desert landscape, with its various cacti and small, shrublike trees, had turned into magnificent pine that shot up to the sky. The more elevation we gained, the more impressive the landscape was. Outside of Tucson, Arizona, close to the Mexican border, the scene could easily be confused with the mountains of Colorado. There was a cool breeze floating down the canyon that provided a pleasing relief to the skin as we pushed our bodies for the second day straight.

The push up to the high pass was the most grueling portion of the trip. The trail was comprised of switchback after switchback all the way up the steep terrain. We had to take regular breaks to ensure we were drinking water and perhaps more importantly, to look around and enjoy the environment. When you are carrying canned goods and gallons of water up a 9,000-foot mountain, your legs will burn. After all these years I can still remember the lactic acid building up in my legs and screaming at my mind for a break. When I felt like I couldn't take another step, I would look at my brothers who were pushing with everything they had. I did not want to be the one who slowed the team down. I knew that if I thought about the outcome, climbing up and then climbing down the other side of the mountain, it would be too much for me to digest. Instead, I suggested that we break for five minutes every hour during our climb. From then on, no matter how bad it hurt, I knew I had a break coming at the end of the hour. "Just get to the break," I told myself. I was showing signs of becoming elite.

Pushing through the leg pain, we continued our climb until we reached the top of the pass. The view of the desert landscape from the top of the mountain was exceptional. I could see all the way to Mexico to the south, and the city of Tucson looked small but beautiful beneath us. Of course, looking out and down was short lived. We were still looking up.

Although we would camp on the pass, the climbing for that day was not yet over. As we stood atop Romero Pass, we saw a beautifully enticing rock shooting up out of the highest point in view. We recognized it as Cathedral Rock, and we had seen it from the base. The thought of being able to climb on a rock that we had talked so much about was too much of temptation for us to resist. We bushwhacked our way up the ridgeline without a trail. It took some time, but there was plenty of daylight. Climbing up the rock freehand, without ropes, was one of the stupidest things I can imagine doing as a kid in junior high. But what can I say – it made sense at the time.

In Over Our Heads

Two of the guys on this trip were brothers and were insepara-ble. On the way up, there was some discussion on which way to approach the rock face. The brothers wanted to go to the left, whereas the others and I wanted to go right. So we separated. My group began climbing up and to the right, and the brothers were soon out of sight. We had chosen a decent line and had numer-ous ledges on which to rest, making a quick climb feasible. We were able to get to the backside and then hike up to the summit.

When I rounded the corner toward the top of cathedral rock, I saw some movement across a canyon. It was the brothers. They had wound up across a vast canyon opposite Cathedral Rock. I yelled out to get their attention, but they were just out of range and could not hear me. They had seen their navigational error and were trying to climb down their side and make it to my location.

The younger brother was in the lead, and he was taking an aggressive route. I noticed that they were standing on a ledge with a snowy slope underneath them. Beyond the snow was a drop off of a couple of hundred feet. My heart sank as I realized that they did not see the cliff ahead of them. More so, the snow we had seen thus far was turned to ice because it was late in the spring. I knew that if he jumped down the ledge and onto the snow, that he would slide down the slope and off the cliff.

My blood turned cold, and my heart was racing. I yelled out as loud as I could to the brothers across the canyon, waving my hands and jumping up and down. "Don't jump," I screamed over and over. My efforts remained unnoticed by the two who were discuss-ing their next move, completely unaware of what the consequence of a poor decision would mean. For me, seeing the big picture and being unable to communicate it to my loved ones was a powerless and frightful feeling. I kept yelling but to no avail. "I'm about to watch my best friend die," I thought as the gravity of the situation sank in. I was still hanging onto the hope that they may turn back in pursuit of a better course when I saw the younger brother look over the edge, bend his knees, and jump down the slope.

Just as I predicted his legs were immediately swept out from underneath him when he landed on the icy slope. He hit his back and began sliding down to his seemingly inevitable death. I was praying out loud in fear, unable to help my friend in any other way. He gained speed and was thrashing around. Just before the edge of the rock cliff, there was a small pine tree sticking out and over the ledge. As the younger brother slid toward the tree, he reached out and hooked it on his arm. It was enough to bring him to a stop just as his legs went over the edge. He was now dangling from an icy cliff, hundreds of feet above the next ledge down.

Nothing compares to helplessly watching a friend in such danger. The younger brother was able to pull himself up, climb back up the ledge, and make it to our location safely. With full knowledge that we almost lost a man at Cathedral Rock, we headed back to the pass to camp before we lost the light.

Final Stretch

The next day we ran out of food and water. The climb down Sabino Canyon was hot and grueling. The pine trees and crisp air quickly digressed into cactus and heat. Without calories to eat and water to drink, it was a game of mental toughness to get down to the trailhead. I remember playing scenes from my favorite movies during the grueling descent. I would imagine Rocky Balboa training in icy Russia in *Rocky IV*. I would often use this strategy when things got tough. The movie scenes have changed over the years, but when you play a movie in your head, time seems to pass without you noticing it.

By that afternoon we were at the trailhead waiting for my mom to pick us up. We had climbed up and down a 9,000-foot mountain, jumped a 55-foot cliff jump, freehand rock climbed Cathedral Rock, nearly lost a friend, exhausted our food and water supply, and perhaps, more important, taken a massive stride into manhood.

The members of that group were elite young men. One of them played semiprofessional baseball, then became a successful entrepreneur; four of us joined the military; and three of us became U.S. Navy SEALs.

Lessons Learned

I know my harrowing "Stand By Me"-style story may have you wondering, "Do you want us to risk our lives?" Of course, that is not my intention with the story. I could have shared numerous stories where the end of the story involved a serene sunset or seeing a bull moose. It just so happens that the stories that I value the most are the ones that excited me the most. My best memories and stories all happened outside. When I can connect with nature, it makes my problems seem small and insignificant. When I have to push past pain to beat the elements, it makes me feel accomplished.

Elite people know how to take situations that should be terrible and make them fun and rewarding by practicing mental toughness strategies. As a junior high student, I learned to make big things small while climbing a mountain. Instead of thinking about the outcome of my goal, I thought about the process. All I had to do was get to the next break, and the rest would take care of itself. When I ran out of food and was on the verge of heat exhaustion, I used thought replacement by playing uplifting movies in my head. I was able to focus on the positive by removing the negativity out of my mind. When I was in pain on the climb, I thought about the needs of my team and didn't want to let them down. Doing so provided me the strength to keep going and the awareness to create a plan that would benefit everyone on my team. I didn't have a book to teach me those things, but I did have experience.

Knowing which tools are in your tool belt is essential. Knowing what tool is right for the job, well that's where the experience comes into play. If you have a broad goal, you can break it down into small goals, at least one of which requires immediate action. Eating an elephant one bite at a time is a mammoth of a task, but you know for a fact that you can take a single bite right now. You just turned something big into something small that you can act on immediately.

Crawl, Walk, Run

I should note that before my parents agreed to the Mount Lemmon climb, they made us camp in the backyard numerous times. They wanted to make sure that I knew how to crawl before I started walking. We did not use anything from inside the house. We burned fire with wood we found and only ate what we took out. After we proved we could crawl, my mom eventually agreed to let us climb a smaller, close to the house mountain called Stafford peak. We climbed it numerous times and always made camp. We had learned how to rely on what was in our backpacks, so this was not over our heads. After showing my parents that I could walk, they were ready to let me run. By the time we were on the large and intimidating Mount Lemmon, we had built multiple benchmarks that made the goal of climbing the mountain attainable. We did it by using the crawl, walk, run benchmarking method (see Figure 4.1).

Think about it this way. I know that the outcome goal is to be able to run. Wanting to run will not make you a good

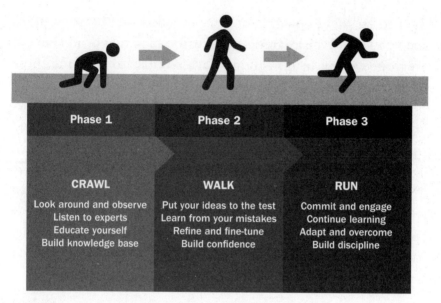

FIGURE 4.1 Crawl, Walk, Run Benchmarking

runner before you have control of your faculties. A one-year-old child can want to run all day but can't until they know how to crawl, stand up, walk, and then begin to run. This process will take years, regardless of the intensity of the desire. Instead of focusing on the outcome, focus on the process. You can set benchmarks that both guide and validate your growth in a specific area. Growth always happens in increments. If you identify your desired outcome and then break it down into separate incremental benchmarks, you will save time, money, and pain. It is possible because you will focus your energy in the right direction and you will give yourself many smaller opportunities to feel successful along the way.

You may have heard the phrase, "death by a thousand cuts." When you focus on the outcome, you will translate setbacks, lost time and effort, and discouragement as a failure. Thousands of less-than-ideal moments will lead you off course and possibly cause you to give up on your vision. If you commit to designing a process that will get you from the crawl stage to the walk stage efficiently, you will find that your self-esteem will increase, your confidence will rise, and you will enjoy the process. Instead of "death by a thousand cuts," it becomes, "success by a thousand small wins."

A few years later, when I found myself at Navy SEAL training, I would think about the benchmarks that I had set in my past that had allowed me to push my limits. During Hell Week I would remind myself that if I had made it over that mountain as a young man, having run out of food and water, then this training should be easy. All I had to do was make it to the next meal. That was more than I had on Mount Lemmon. When I was ambushed in the Middle East, I thought about how I made it through Hell Week, so this should be easy.

When we push ourselves past our comfort zone, we are creating mental benchmarks that can be relied on when things get tough. These experiences show us what we are capable of. We can apply a process that worked in another context to our current problem and use it against that problem to assert our will.

Becoming Elite!

1. Set benchmarks to "crawl, walk, run" your way to success.
2. Use movies that have inspired you as a form of thought replacement. I highly recommend *Rocky IV*!
3. Don't focus on the outcome of your goals. Focus on the process that is necessary to achieve your goal and practice using it.

Choosing the Warrior Mentality

A warrior mentality is a critical component of becoming elite. One of the key characteristics of elite people is that they refuse to be victimized. The world is not happening to them. They are happening to the world. Warriors are not victims. In fact, you cannot be both at the same time. You must choose. This choice is one you must make every day. Will you be a victim or will you be a warrior? I can certainly admit that I've had a couple of moments in life when that was a hard choice to make.

Marathon Is Half the Word

A few years ago my wife and I spent a year in Montana. We had two kids at the time – one was three years old, and one was one. My wife had been wanting to fulfill her lifelong dream of running a half marathon. Neither of us had been running as part of our workout routine, so she had a long way to go. I had a long way to go as well but did not share the same passion as her and have always hated running. Although I wasn't going to run the half marathon with my wife, I did want to support her in whatever way possible.

The best way to support a mother is to offer to watch the kids. That is the single most helpful thing that a father can do for a mother, besides maybe the dishes. But I wasn't satisfied with merely watching the kids. I wanted to take on a more significant role. So I decided to pull out an old skill set that I hadn't used for some time, one that I had developed in my younger years and was actually quite good at. Rollerblading is a skill that is not always popular in terns of social convention, but that didn't matter. I was helping my wife.

So I went to the sporting goods store and bought a pair of rollerblades! That's right, a beautiful pair of K2 inline skates. I was so excited because I finally found an excuse to do it. And, of course, I would play the martyr card in an effort to garner the support of my friends.

"It's a perfect idea," I thought as I prepared the double stroller for action. The kids would sit in their prospective seats, tied in for safety. I was going to be flying down the road after all. I fastened a Bluetooth speaker to the crossbar and found the perfect Internet radio station. Me, my wife, my two kids, and Marky Mark and the Funky Bunch were about to kick some serious ass!

My wife, the good sport that she is, humored the idea. We set out on a long run, or in my case, roll. We were in an area of Montana that sat deep in the valley, so the hills did not prove challenging. The kids loved it, not as much as me, but they looked forward to the runs. As she trained for the marathon, the training runs became longer and longer. We would park in town, next to a good restaurant, and then take off on a big loop that ended back at the car. The reward for our trouble was an excellent cheat meal. We were both burning calories, and hey, we deserved it.

Finally came race day. The plan was to drive my wife to the buses so that she could register. Then I would take the kids to the starting line to watch their mom be awesome. On the way to the starting line, I stopped at a convenience store because it was early and I needed a pick-me-up. I grabbed a frothy mocha frappuccino and smoked a cigar while the kids rested in the car. After I finished my morning beverage, I loaded up the kids in the stroller and walked to the starting line.

The place was electric. Speakers were blaring music while the participants warmed up. It felt more like six o'clock in the afternoon than six o'clock in the morning. I was so moved by the energy level that I couldn't help but think about how I had the kids in the stroller already. The stroller was prepared and guess what? My rollerblades were sitting in the lower pouch, beckoning me to put them on. And I would. Unregistered, untrained, and perhaps unwanted, I set up my rollerblades and prepared for total domination! I would support my wife by working as her pit crew. I could carry her energy gels and her water while providing her with the soothing sounds of Marky Mark. Yes, friends, it was indeed perfect.

Fireworks went off as the gun fired signaling the beginning of the race. I was unable to strap on my rollerblades because of the sheer number of people. Instead, I would blend in with them, run for a mile or so then pull over to don my skates of steel. So I ran. The road was packed. So I ran some more. It would take more than a mile. Toward mile two, my wife asked if she could run ahead, unencumbered by the stroller. I told her that I would quickly catch her once the crowd thinned and I could strap on my blades. In truth, I was relieved because remember that cigar and frappuccino that I had unknowingly enjoyed not an hour before? Yeah, milk was a bad choice! My stomach gurgled with furious anger. It bellowed as if to warn me of the carnage to come. And moments later the warning was fulfilled – on the road, with runners all around, and my kids to watch.

I needed to put some distance between myself and ground zero. So I ran. To my surprise, I felt much better. It was a slight downhill, and the weight of my stroller was carrying me, and my stomach felt the sweet release of emptiness. Another mile came and went as I waited for my moment.

The people stayed crowded together. There were pit stops everywhere and security placed intermittently. I couldn't help but think that when I strapped on my rollerblades that I might be asked to leave or even chased off the course. What kind of example would that be for my new found fans? I would wait for another mile or so at least until it thinned out even more.

At the pit stops, the helpers would see me pushing two kids in a stroller and yell amazing things to me. They shouted, "Superdad!" "You have some lucky kids," one yelled. This became the norm. Even other runners would say encouraging words as they passed me. I realized something unusual at that moment. I had fans. They loved me. So I ran. I couldn't let my fans down after all. They needed me, and I needed them. It was around mile seven when I finally realized that I was running a damned marathon! Well, half marathon. Besides if I were to put on my rollerblades now, I may be asked to leave. And the truth is, once you're halfway through a half marathon, you really need to finish, because when will you ever be halfway through a half marathon again? That is like a quarter of a marathon, after all.

Pushing the stroller filled with water, needless equipment, and two kids, I pushed on. The energy of the event carried me forward. I wasn't even in pain until about mile eleven. People who train for marathons refer to something known as "the wall." For runners, this will happen around mile twenty. For out-of-shape fathers pushing strollers, I can honestly say it happens much quicker. My pace slowed, and my feet got sloppy. They began dragging and felt like cement. I pushed on and dug deep. My heart lifted when I finally saw the finish line ahead.

There was a bridge that went over the city with the large finish line just past it. I could hear music and an announcer saying everyone's name who crossed the finish line. The announcements were possible because, at registration, participants were given trackers to put on their shoes. I, of course, was not an official participant and had no such tracker. As I approached the finish line, I heard them say the name of the person to my far left side. Then another name to my immediate left. Then the announcer said, "And to the far right we have . . ." – crickets. They knew. The truth is, when you're as completely exhausted as

I was in that moment, you don't care. I saw a woman handing out finisher medals, and I went straight up to her, bowed my head like Lancelot after a joist, and she placed the medal over my head and said: "Congratulations, you're Superdad."

At that moment something swelled in my heart. I felt butterflies in my stomach. For a moment it could have been pride or a sense of accomplishment. In the next moment, the feeling in my stomach felt more acidic as my body felt hot. Not a few seconds after the woman placed the medal on my head, I hurled. All over the road by the finish line. And not just once, it went on for some time. It felt like an eternity anyway. I would lose my stomach three more times that morning. If there is one thing that I learned, it is that people forgive a father who goes the extra 13.1 miles for their kids, rollerblades or not.

Be Better Today Than Yesterday

You might be wondering, "what lessons can we learn from a man on rollerblades pushing kids in a stroller?" It is not the action that matters here but rather the mentality behind the lesson. In the SEAL teams, we had a standard that we held one another accountable too. One of the messages was to "Earn your trident everyday." It means that to be elite, you must not rest on the accomplishments of yesterday. You are as good as you are today. You are not done growing. You still have to earn your spot every single day. Too often, people hit a benchmark or achieve an accomplishment and stop. This is true with people from all walks of life and various backgrounds. They settle into comfort because they have already accomplished what they initially set out to do. They stop growing.

I once saw this exemplified before my eyes with an old friend from high school. I had not heard from him in over a decade, and he reached out to reconnect. Naturally, I went to his Facebook page to see what he had been up to, quickly realizing that he had not been up to much over the past 10 years. His background image on the account was a picture of him playing football in high school. This surprised me. He was a talented guy who could have done anything he wanted with this life, but I couldn't help but feel sad for him. Was the most significant thing that he had accomplished in life over before he turned 18? Was this the best image he would ever have of himself? Why would he be looking back when there was still so much time to live in front of him? I did not understand it at the time. It wasn't until I got out of the military and moved into the next phase of life that I began to understand the dynamic that had crippled my old friend from moving on to his true potential.

Almost a Victim

When I got out of the SEAL teams, I quickly learned that things would be different from then on. I would deploy for a couple of months and then return home. While at home, I had no office to check into, no one checking up on me, and nothing to do but spend time with family. At first, I enjoyed the freedom. I could work out whenever it made sense, spend my time hiking in the mountains, and put my kids to bed in the evening. Of course, after a couple of months, when I started missing my friends and the excitement of working overseas, I would return to work.

Everything was working out quite nicely until one day I was injured. Not stub-your-toe hurt, but life-changing injured. I smashed a disk in my spine and was unable to be a useful member of the team. My whole purpose of being overseas was to carry people out of dangerous situations if needed and I couldn't even walk to the chow hall for a meal. I flew home, and although

I didn't know it then, that was my last time I would ever deploy. I ended up with spinal fusion surgery on my L5-S1 vertebrae that left me useless for a year. I was unable to lift more than a few pounds, let alone work out. I could not carry my children, let alone a gun. I had lost my job, my physicality, my purpose, and most importantly, my *identity*.

For my entire professional life, I had been an operator. I was a Navy SEAL, at the top of my game, then a contractor for an elite unit, and now I was reduced to asking my wife to help me after using the restroom. I couldn't even do that. Quickly, my muscles began to atrophy. I started looking weak and frail. Eventually, my midsection began to grow due to inactivity, a poor diet, and way too much alcohol. I was drinking a lot of whiskey because I refused to take the pain medication for more than a few weeks after the surgery. I had seen what pills do to people and wanted no part of it, but the bottle was beginning to seem like a lateral move.

Everything hurt. My back was in severe pain. As a result of atrophy, my stabilization muscles were almost nonexistent. The result was that all those injuries acquired over the years of abusing my body began to flare up. My shoulders, my wrists, ankles, and neck were all in pain. Everything hurt, but nothing more than my pride. I had lost one of the central pieces in my life that defined me as an individual. I had been climbing a ladder my whole life, and I had just slipped. I lost my handhold and had fallen to the last rung and was hanging on with one hand. There was a choice in front of me. Would I continue to be a warrior, or had that all changed? I could admit that life had beaten me up–there is no harm in that after all, life beats up people all the time. Every prizefighter gets knocked out eventually, right? What's the harm in admitting that? It is normal. Its expected. I could merely accept my new life as a victim, or I could step up.

Look Forward, Not Back

I could be a victim, or I could earn my trident that day. I could continue to earn my trident every day after that. I was still the same person I had always been. The guy who laughed with his buddies after not sleeping for well over five days, the guy who made a joke when under attack at six o'clock in the morning, the guy who could get knocked around and always get back up. I was still me. Navy SEAL was just one thing that I had done. It was a part of me, but it was not my identity. Working in the Middle East was a rewarding experience, but I didn't need to be capable of that work anymore because I could find something new. I could choose never to be a victim and always to be my true self, a warrior – a man who could look the demon in the face and laugh, a guy who would die trying if you gave him a chance.

Looking backward, to the past can be a dangerous thing. When you are driving down the highway in your car, you look through the windshield. It is a large window so that you can capture everything that is coming at you. The rearview mirror, on the other hand, is small and out of the way. Sure, it is there in case you need a quick reference, but you can't look at it too long without getting into trouble. When you are cruising down the road, objects are coming at you quickly. You have to have your eyes on the road so that you can read the environment and then react appropriately. If you stare at the rearview mirror the whole time, you will likely wreck the car and not get to where you want to go.

Elite people know that the future is coming at them quickly. The past is there for reference sure, but that road is gone, and there is a new road ahead. You will never get to where you want to be in life if you are obsessed with the past. You can shape your future. If you commit to being better today than you were yesterday, to not allowing your past to dictate your future, then you will be amazed at your increased ability and overall happiness. It's time to get your eyes back on the road and hit the accelerator!

My Accelerator Moment

I committed to my family and myself that I would not become that overweight, washed up, unhealthy alcoholic, who *used* to be a Navy SEAL. My Facebook page would not have a picture of me in my prime for the next 40 years. I would not live my life trying to drive while staring at the rearview mirror. I would keep my eyes on the road. I would charge on, and I would take back my life.

For the next long while, I would repeat those words in my head every morning, "Earn your trident every day." When physical therapy got tough, I would repeat those words to myself. When I wanted to get drunk and forget about life, when I wanted to crawl into a hole and hide I would tell myself, "Earn it." When I wanted to hide from the pain and take some pills, I would tell myself, "Earn it." The trident was more than something that I had worn on my chest. It was my symbol of being better than the challenges I faced, of never giving up. It was a constant reminder that it doesn't matter what I did yesterday; all that matters is who I am today. My identity was more than being a Navy SEAL. My identity was rooted in being a warrior who was committed to being better today than he was yesterday. No one could take that part of me away from me.

Be 1% Better Every Day

My life-changing injury set me back, but not for long. I had been around elite people for my entire professional life and knew that my situation was temporary. I could improve myself slowly so long as I stayed committed to doing so. We call this Incremental Improvement. I can't lose 30 pounds in a day. It takes time. One trick of the elite is to improve 1% every day. By incrementally improving, we can make change and growth a sustainable part of our lives.

Your current position in this world, your body's health, your career, and your reputation are all the sum of millions of small decisions made over time. Those decisions either lead to improvement or decay. Consider this; there is no organism on this planet that is static or stationary. Everything is either growing or dying. Sure, it's slow, but their direction is consistent. Every single one of your decisions are either leading to your growth or your decline.

This idea led to the discovery of the aggregation of marginal gains. The concept is credited to a UK cycling coach named Sir Dave Brailsford and is rooted in how growing by 1% every day leads to significant improvements over more extended periods of time. This model works because the 1% is not a static number; it is 1% of the whole. Tomorrow that 1% will be of greater value than today's 1%. Over time, that 1% will begin to represent much more substantial growth. As you see in Figure 5.1, giving a single percentage point of additional effort every day leads to exponential returns on your investment.

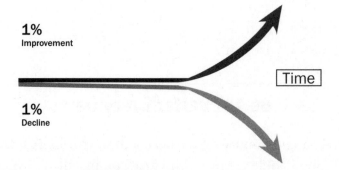

FIGURE 5.1 Aggregation of Marginal Gains

I knew that I was not ready to start running after my surgery, but I wanted to support my wife. By rollerblading for weeks to support her, let's call that 1%, I was able to build up my cardiovascular shape and strengthen the muscles in my legs and back. My hips regained some of their mobility as my athleticism came back to me slowly. I was improving incrementally by way of smaller, more attainable goals. By the time I was at the race, my body was able to perform, and I completed a half marathon. I had no idea that I could do it until it was already happening. The incremental improvement was so natural and mostly unnoticed that I surprised even myself. If your goal is to lose weight, you must be diligent to guard your mind against discouragement. I hate to be the one to break it to you, but you will not look like an underwear model in two weeks. Instead, focus on what 1% looks like over time. If you sit during the day, take a walk at lunch. If your friends from the office go out to eat at lunch, make sure to order a healthier option than you did yesterday.

In the same way, if you are performing at a high level and you are not sure how to bust through a growth plateau, think about dividing your life into different segments. If one of those segments is lifelong learning, consider how you can grow by one percent in that specific area. Listening to an audiobook on your commute might be the answer. Next week, it may be in the selection of what audiobook to listen to. Before you know it, you are knocking out books left and right, and applying that knowledge directly to other areas of your life.

You do not have to build Rome in a day, lose all your weight immediately, or produce a PhD by tomorrow to become elite. All you have to do is commit to becoming 1% better today than you were yesterday. This is the mentality of a warrior. You are not a victim. You have a warrior's mindset hell-bent on improving every day so that you can leave your mark on this world.

Becoming Elite!

1. Your identity is not a position or title.
2. You are not a victim, and this life is not happening to you. You are happening to it.
3. Identify areas for improvement and be 1% better tomorrow than you are today.
4. Get your eyes off the rearview mirror and back on the road because you have places to go.

Be Self-Aware

We've all been there. You're at a movie, trying to enjoy your popcorn and a good flick. The room goes dark, and it's perfectly quiet as words on a blackened screen begin to tell you the timeframe and setting of the movie. Just then, like lightning cracking, the guy in the row behind you starts opening the tinfoil-like packaging on his candy. Okay, understandable – annoying, but understandable. A rational human being would only take about five seconds to open a candy wrapper, but sadly, that is not the case in this movie theater. The invisible menace behind you spends what seems like an hour making the horrifically distracting noise. As if that's not enough, he begins eating the candy, if *eating* is even the word. He smashes and destroys the candy viciously between his mighty jaws, all the while keeping his mouth wide open so the sound of the carnage booms through all of eternity.

As he smacks in your ear, you wonder what went wrong with this man's childhood? Was he abandoned on the doorstep of the fire department and then found by wolves before firefighters could come to rescue him? Did he escape from the confines of North Korea as a boy? Was he involved in a shipwreck, leaving him stranded for months floating atop the ocean in a dinghy with a giant tiger on board? How does a person remain so clueless about how he's severely hampering the cinematic experience of the people around him? It's a classic case of the person who lacks self-awareness.

Self-awareness provides a significant advantage for the person who desires to be elite. When we know where we are and what we are lacking, it's easy to see where we can improve. Conversely, if we are unaware of our current state, then our efforts at self-improvement would essentially be nothing more than shots fired in the dark. We have all gone through situations where we overvalued our contributions. Usually, this is a result of our youth. When I look back on some of the stupid stuff that I've done, I cringe. I cringe because I've grown up and matured past the person I used to be. When I was a child, I acted like a child. Now, as a man, I'm committed to an effort to become a better version of myself every day.

This effort must start with the understanding of the personality type that we default to naturally. We all default to different states. Some people are naturally more aggressive than others. Some keep their cool with little effort and let the problems of the world wash over them. Others are loud and boisterous, commanding every room they enter, whereas others still are deep thinking, quiet, and reflective, extracting truths from daily happenings in an effort to create. We are all different, and that difference is where our beauty, as a species, lies. We should celebrate this fact, but this will only be possible once we understand it. Our understanding will work in two different ways. First, we will become self-aware, which will allow us to celebrate our strengths and mitigate the adverse effects of the weaknesses contained within our nature. The second is that we will come to value and appreciate people around us that are different than we are because they are strong in the areas that we are weak.

What Is Your Personality Type?

There have been many personality tests published over the centuries to help us understand our natural default state better. In the past few decades, it has become an essential part of any business school graduate program. These tests have many classifications and blends of classifications and are quite intricate and too complicated to understand. For our purposes, let's explore the simplest form of personality classifications described

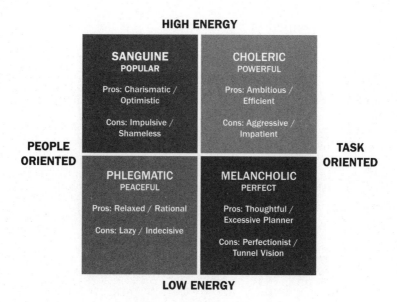

FIGURE 6.1   Four Temperaments

by the Greek physician Hippocrates as the four temperaments (see Figure 6.1).

Although this wisdom comes to us from 400 BC, it does a beautiful job of illustrating personality traits from an observational level while also illustrating certain downfalls that can be harmful. As you read this, I invite you to think about which of these is your default state. Given the proper social structure and situational context, we can rise to the challenge of adapting our behavior to what is required.

Don't be too concerned with that right now. Instead, think about what you are when you have the choice, what you are when nobody's watching, and what you are when you are not thinking about what you should be. As you read these, please keep in mind that there is no right answer. Elite people come from all four categories, and elite teams will usually include multiple types. There is no judgment here, just a better understanding of your natural tendencies.

Choleric

Pros: The choleric person is one who dots his lowercase j's. They are usually more organized than others and prefer others to be similar to them in this regard. They tend to be ambitious and passionate, believing that their way is more than likely the better way, so there is no need to see how others have done it in the past. Despite that fact, they are still efficient. Their confidence comes from their ability to plan and solve problems, and they have a strong history of being right. They can most certainly delegate, but strong oversight is necessary for the best result. Their leadership quality and assertiveness can serve them well in an emergency as long as there is a firm plan in place. They're often drawn to roles of leadership and can make excellent producers and builders.

Cons: Unfortunately, there is always a catch. Without self-awareness, the ambition of the choleric can turn into a domineering, overly aggressive person. They can be quite impatient and rude. Their belief that they are usually right can also make them argumentative and intolerant. The real problem is that they often judge people too harshly who aren't the same personality type and then hate others who are the same for continually challenging them. The result is often a tendency to micromanage. As leaders, they often demand loyalty while not having much empathy for those they lead.

Sanguine

Pros: You will identify the sanguine personality immediately after they walk into the room, as their charisma will instantaneously fill the room. They can command attention with their fun-loving and optimistic outlook spoken with many words at a loud volume. Their warm-hearted nature makes them quick to apologize and excellent at making friends. They are prone to spontaneity and will do anything in their power to prevent dull moments. People are excited when they come around, but, sometimes, good things are better in smaller doses. They are drawn to roles that involve selling, acting, and speaking publicly. Other people may try to get out of the spotlight. The sanguine personality embraces it. If you have ever referred to someone as being very charismatic, you may have been talking about a sanguine personality.

Cons: When spontaneity becomes impulsive, people can get hurt. They create such a powerful first impression that letting people down can become second nature. They can struggle with habitual tardiness and will blow off tasks that are boring. They will exaggerate the story if it means they will achieve a better response or a louder laugh. They can become extraordinarily self-absorbed and seem always to have a good reason when things go wrong.

Phlegmatic

Pros: This is a person who prides himself in staying relaxed and calm, regardless of his surroundings. They are very consistent and content with who they are. They can be quite affectionate and are excellent at keeping the peace. Their diplomatic nature allows them to make friends quickly. They are rational and prefer a more utilitarian view of ethics, meaning that they will lean toward a decision that provides the greatest good for the greatest number of people. They are very observant, but the problems of this world can flow over them like water, having little effect. They can do this because they are prone to keeping things in perspective. In a crisis, they perform very well and usually keep their cool. They are attracted to the roles of diplomats, accountants, teachers, and technicians – or any other position that allows them to thrive in a volatile environment.

Cons: As you can imagine, someone who is very content is also prone to laziness. They can be indecisive and passive-aggressive. Goal setting is not natural for them and they will often over-compromise in relationships, giving up too much of who they are and what they value, leading to discouragement and communicating through sarcasm.

Melancholic

Pros. Finally, we have the melancholic. These people are incredibly thoughtful and considerate. Everything on this planet has a meaning that is deeper than superficial observation. They are very cautious and often empathetic of others. They are schedule oriented and quite detailed in their planning. Their foresight makes them excellent at preventing future problems. Their most noticeable quality is the ability of expression beyond the verbal. They are excellent creators of content, poetry, and art. They are independent in their thinking, finding their meaning in this world and for this world. They prefer roles of artists, musicians, inventors, philosophers, and doctors.

Cons: As with any creator, they can often be obsessive about their work. This obsessiveness can consume them for long periods of time and lead to moodiness and depression. They can also be perfectionists and very self-critical. They are often pessimistic and difficult to please. Tragedy affects them profoundly and can take more time to get over than those around them. Although they are known for their tunnel vision, they are often prone to procrastination. If you find people who are prone to play the martyr, they're probably melancholic.

Know Where You're Coming From

I'm sure that as you were reading these descriptions, you couldn't help but think of people you know, your family members, and even your boss. It is always easier to identify other people's strengths and weaknesses than it is our own. For this reason, you may want to get a few other people to tell you which of the four temperaments they think you are and then decide for yourself. Of course, if while reading the cons of one of those temperaments stung a little, that might be a good sign that you are identifying with that temperament on a subconscious level.

Knowledge is power. There are pieces of you that are brilliant and add value to any group or situation that you have. Knowing where to apply yourself for the maximum payout could prove beneficial for the entrepreneur deciding which industry to choose and for the company man who can select assignments. As a leader, it will help you choose the members of your team as well. If you select people who are strong where you are weak, then your team will be better balanced and prepared to handle a variety of work.

For that reason, knowing your weakness will enhance your ability to lead and make decisions. If you are a sanguine personality who is prone to being impulsive, then you will know not to hit Send after you compose a tweet about someone who wronged you. Instead, you can implement a personal policy that involves a commitment never to send a message while you are still angry. Save it as a draft and wait until the next morning to reread the tweet and make sure that it serves the interests of both you and your team.

Remember, just because your natural temperament comes with specific weaknesses and pitfalls does not necessarily mean that you have to be limited by them. You can train yourself away from your weaknesses, chipping away at them bit by bit. You can place the chisel on the jagged edges apparent from birth and let the hammer drop. You can take the negative aspects of your nature out of your backpack and leave them on the ground. Doing so will enable you to build a future with the positive influence of self awareness.

Play Well with Others

A wise man once told me, "Expect a fox to act like a fox and expect a scorpion to act like a scorpion." If I know that I'm dealing with a scorpion, then it's impossible to be disappointed when it attempts to strike me with its poisonous tail. The thought of yelling out in pain, "I trusted you, scorpion! I thought we were friends!" is both comical and ridiculous.

Not to accuse any one temperament listed earlier to be that of a scorpion or fox, but correctly identifying what you are dealing with can undoubtedly serve to mitigate disappointment. When you can identify someone's personality type and then realize that he or she has embraced the wrong characteristics of their nature, you can anticipate future interactions.

One thing that I have improved upon in recent years is the ability to identify the personality types of the people I work with and then use that when building effective teams. The SEAL teams taught me the value of inclusion. When creating a SEAL platoon, the leadership chooses people who are subject-matter experts in different fields of expertise. Yes, we need a few snipers, but a platoon built entirely of snipers would not be ideal because it would limit the overall capability of the team. Instead, we have a sniper, a communications expert, an explosive breacher, and so on.

We all have different strengths, but the word diversity still falls short. We do not see it as being different but rather as being specialized. Incorporating multiple specializations in a team is an idea called inclusion. People do not want to get a job because of the diversity that they bring. Professionals want to receive the position because they are great at what they do. We are not different. We are specialized.

When I can identify a person as a choleric personality, for example, it makes it easy to understand when they become impatient or display a lack of empathy. It also brings clarity to your decision when it is time to delegate a task. For example, if it's exciting and involves being in the public eye, then it may be a better task for a sanguine personality, rather than a phlegmatic personality.

When you are developing a younger, inexperienced member of your team who happens to be a melancholic, it may be beneficial to nurture their attention to detail while letting them know that there is no reason to be so hard on themselves. When you know their default state, your ability to nurture the good and mitigate the negative will make you a better leader, teammate, and even friend.

Knowing your personality and your natural tendencies will make it easier for you to build your personal policy and make plans explicitly catered to you. Additionally, it will help you figure out what types of people you should surround yourself with. Think about your weaknesses and what personality types will best fill those gaps. Learn to see the value in other people's strengths and how to help them fill their gaps. Remember, you are not different; you are specialized.

Becoming Elite!

1. Think about the personality type you suspect you might be. Ask three friends if they agree.
2. Write down three strengths that you have as a direct result of your personality type. Then write down ways that you can use those strengths to grow as a person and a professional.

(continued)

3. Write down three weaknesses that are a direct result of your personality type. Then write down some personal policies that will help you minimize the downside of these tendencies.

4. Define your most significant gaps and what personality type would best help you fill those gaps. Think about how you can apply this to your personal life as well as your professional team.

Surround Yourself with the Right People

The famous author and celebrated speaker Jim Rohn famously said, "We are the average of the five people that we spend the most time with." If you spend time with elite people, you will always be challenged to grow and improve. Elite people find ways of making those around them elite. If you are wondering how this works, let me explain. If I have a cup of hot coffee and I drop an ice cube in it, both the ice cube and the coffee will begin to change. The ice cube will melt, and the coffee will become cooler. The temperatures of both objects equalize.

People behave similarly. If you decide to set a New Year's resolution of running a half marathon or rollerblading in one for argument's sake, then you are like the hot coffee. You are burning with excitement to accomplish a challenging task and ready to start training. If you have five friends who are couch potatoes by day and bar room heroes by night, you just dropped five ice cubes in your coffee. Whether you like it or not, those ice cubes will affect your passion, drive, and commitment to accomplishing your goal of running a half marathon.

Now imagine this: You are taking your time drinking your morning coffee. You notice that it is cooled off a bit. You boil some water and add the boiling water to your coffee. The two temperatures equalize and bring your cup of coffee back to an enjoyable temperature for drinking. Imagine how much better your odds will be of accomplishing your marathon dreams if you surround yourself with people who will add heat to your flame. Look for active friends if you want people in your life who can hold you accountable when your motivation is low. If you know people who have run multiple marathons in the past, you will have guidance when you make decisions on your training program, what you eat the night before a race, how to use mental toughness techniques when you are exhausted. The point is this: If you surround yourself with people of elite desire, elite knowledge, and elite work ethic, you will become elite.

It Starts with Authenticity

The elite professional football coach John Madden once said, "If you want longevity in this league, first you must be authentic." People have a knack for identifying a fake. Street smarts refer to our basic ability to notice the true intentions of others, recognize patterns, and ultimately survive. It is an innate quality that exists on the most basic human level. When your purposes are entirely selfish, the street-smart individual will sniff you out. You cannot fake sincerity for long. Being sincere requires a certain level of honesty and vulnerability that can be uncomfortable, but after a time, you become comfortable with the honest, true self you are sharing with others. Faking sincerity takes a lot of work and eventually wears you out. In short, you have to be real. Plus, you will find it liberating. You owe it to yourself to be happy, and when you are your genuine self, you will feel more at peace then if you were to fake it.

Think of it as a first date. You can easily pretend to be something you are not, but who are you hurting? The other person is going to realize your true self at some point in time. It may take a month, year, or even 10 years of marriage, but eventually, you will be found out. Why waste your valuable time? If you are genuinely yourself on a first date, then you may find that the other person likes the real you. Why would you ever want to spend time and money on someone who only likes a manufactured reflection of who you are?

Elite relationships are best when built on the foundation of a genuine connection of trust. Remember, being authentic equals longevity. So be yourself and stick around for a while.

Relationships: The Expanding Circle

Our relationships come in three different categories. You'll notice in Figure 7.1 that the circles represent three types of relationships. The largest circle is your expanding circle, which represents your network – the people you know from professional commonalities. They may be from work, school, or events designed to drive business. The middle circle is your personal board of advisors. These are people whose time is valuable, so you can't share every detail of your life, but whose commitment to you is beyond that of an acquaintance from your network. Next, we see the inner circle. These are the people with whom you can share the nuances of your life, the good and bad details. These are people that you trust above all others and keep close. Your inner circle may include your spouse, best friends, or old

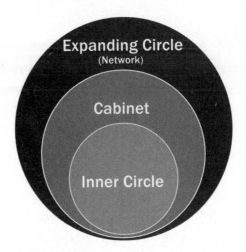

FIGURE 7.1 Expanding Circle

classmates from school. Now, let's discuss how to be proactive about selecting the people that we want to allow into our three circles.

Remember that it is both your choice and your responsibility to make sure that you are allowing the right people into your circle. Do not allow ice cubes into your hot coffee. When building your network, you should always try and surround yourself with those with whom you respect and genuinely want to connect. Chances are, the feeling is mutual. Start making friends with people who will motivate you, can mentor you, or keep you in check. Build a foundation of trust so that the relationship that will last.

Avoid looking for people who are just like you; instead, look for people who value you for who you are and believe in your aspirations. If they are a different personality type, make sure that they appreciate you for your strengths. Try not to see them as different but as specialized. Their point of view may illuminate something that you have not yet seen. Value diversity in your selections. They add value with actionable advice because they trust and believe in you.

Network: Your Expanding Circle

It is true that you are as strong as your network. The people that you know will dramatically shape what you think and what you do. From employment to personal influence, your ability to network will have a profound effect on your life. The problem is that while we are all reading the same word, "networking," it means different things to different people.

Have you ever been to a networking event and noticed people using it as a sales call? They are always promoting their services or product instead of connecting with people. In fact, you may see people actively avoiding them. Most people don't want to be sucked into a conversation with a person who is not being real.

Many people come across as used car salesmen in their communication, both digitally and in person. It happens all the time, and not always for terrible reasons. Usually, it is the result of time allocation. We are all busy, and finding time for all the requirements of home, work, and personal well-being make building a network seem time consuming. Often we cut things down to the basic needs of our professional lives, which usually means a bottom line. The fact is that if you approach a networking event as a sales call, you will not be able to build lasting relationships.

A better approach is to take the word *networking* out of your vocabulary altogether. It applies a scientific approach to something that should be organic and genuine. Start thinking about it as your expanding circle. It is still a circle of friends, but it is one that you can afford to expand because it requires little time to keep intact. If your expanding circle consists of people who you connect with on a level deeper than the "bottom line," you will notice that months or even years can go by without costing you the relationship.

An excellent way to make sure that you are creating a network built for the long haul is to be mindful of what you are asking people to give up. Instead of asking for business or a sale, ask for knowledge. Asking others for information has two beneficial effects. The first is that it gets others talking about themselves, which makes them feel valued. The second is that most people are happy giving away information for free. They guard their money but freely share their knowledge. Feel free to chime in when you agree or disagree as well. The aim should be a fruitful, mutually beneficial conversation.

When you are communicating with your expanding circle, remember this. People will forget a majority of the data contained within the conversation. They will, however, remember the way the discussion made them feel. You will notice this to be true for all communication. When people think of you in the future, when they are deciding whether or not to pick up the phone or return a text, they will remember the way you made them feel. Treat them with respect and provide a stimulating conversation and you will gain access to other elite people who will be proud to be in your expanding circle.

Middle Circle: Personal Board of Advisors

Accountability breeds response-ability.

– Stephen Covey

Since separating from the military, I have identified a need to bring people on as advisors in my life. In the military the rules are different, and those rules do not apply nearly as much out here in the world. I quickly realized that I needed help to make the transition as smooth as possible. I needed to establish my middle circle, a personal board of advisors (PBA). I see it in the same light as the president of the United States sees his own cabinet or a company's board of advisors. I have a small group of individuals who have become trusted friends, whom I have allowed into my life.

Although I may seem outgoing, I'm really quite private. Allowing people to see me, the good and the bad (and even the ugly), has been a challenge, but it has also yielded significant results. I've been able to consider a wide array of input on various professional and personal decisions in my life, and it has produced excellent results.

Think about what type of people you want to put in your advisory board. I highly recommend a diverse group of people with various strengths, with plenty of experience, and who have made sound decisions themselves.

I don't know your particular situation, what your decisions will entail, or your constraints. What I will say is this: diversify. When you're building a stock portfolio, you have a distribution of investments categorized by those with high risk and those with low risk. As I'm sure you know, this is the definition of diversification. If all of your holdings are bonds, you don't risk your life savings, but you also have no hope of a high return. Conversely, if you're only investing in startups hoping they become a proverbial rocket ship, you're taking an incredible risk, and you could lose it all, but there's also a chance you'll reap extremely high rewards. A solid financial plan involves using both strategies simultaneously. By diversifying your portfolio, you can enjoy the peace of having some safety and stability built into your plan while still accepting some risk for a healthy return. Why not apply this same practice to your personal advisory board?

Choose one person who is inclined to give bold advice – a risk taker who doesn't mind shooting for the stars and has demonstrated his own ability to do so. To balance that individual out, choose another person who prefers a more stable strategy designed to provide a modest return over time without accepting much risk. The advice that these two individuals give you will present two opposing viewpoints that you can learn from.

Inner Circle: Your Friends

Like a bouncer at the local club, you are responsible for maintaining the proper occupancy limit of your middle circle. You need to be selective about the people you let in. These people should be fun, have a positive mindset, and genuinely care about you and your well-being. If you want to be an active person, then surround yourself with other active people. If you desire stimulating conversations, then find people who enjoy conversing and are not easily offended by open discussion. If you like to laugh, find funny people that add levity to your life. Remember, you will slowly become like these people so be deliberate with your selections. Be deliberate, but not selfish.

You may see other people who need your influence to better their own lives. Do not shy away from these individuals just because you are strong where they are weak. Instead, pour some boiling water into their coffee. Lift them up to your level and become a positive influence in their lives.

Don't get carried away though. You are still the bouncer of the club. Some people will do more harm than good. These people have no place in the life of an elite person. If you allow negative, cynical, self-defeating people into your middle circle, they will feed your negative demon. They will suck the life out of you and make you doubt yourself.

Negativity spreads like cancer. It will infect you and the others in your circle in time. There is only one way to deal with cancer. You have to perform surgery and remove it. Yes, surgery is tough, and recovery is painful, but it is better than dying of cancer.

In Practice

Now that you've established your three circles, you can start using these relationships to better your life and to make better decisions. For example, when faced with a choice that's left you feeling uneasy, it's essential that you spend some time in reflection. You need to understand the details of your situation before you communicate it to your PBA because it is important to be respectful of their time. These are elite people after all, and they may have a lot on their plate. One way to do this is by working through a root cause analysis, which is a way of

A Five Whys Worksheet

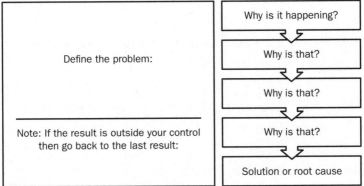

Define the problem:

Note: If the result is outside your control then go back to the last result:

Why is it happening?

Why is that?

Why is that?

Why is that?

Solution or root cause

FIGURE 7.2   Root Cause Analysis, "Five Whys"

sorting through the symptoms of a problem to discover the actual cause or root.

A useful technique that will help you with this called the "Five Whys" (see Figure 7.2). It works like this. Get in a room with your inner circle and use a whiteboard to write down your problem. Then, ask yourself why that problem exists. Your answer will be a symptom, not the cause. Ask why that symptom exists and write it down next to the first symptom. If your team asks five whys to a problem, you will likely discover the root cause of that problem. Do not be afraid to go past five when it is necessary. Now, you have identified something that is worth taking to your Personal Board of Advisors to discuss possible solutions.

Here is an example of a problem that a head coach of an athletic team may have:

Problem: My team is not winning games

Why? Because my players are not finishing strong.
Why? Because they lose their heart in the fourth quarter.

Why? Because they get tired and think about themselves.

Why? Because they are playing for themselves, not for each other.

Why? Because I have created a culture that focuses on the individual more than the team.

Here is another example that a project manager may have in a corporation:

Problem: We are behind schedule

Why? Because my personnel are missing deadlines.

Why? Because they are making too many mistakes.

Why? Because they hear conflicting information from different sources.

Why? Because they do not know who to listen to.

Why? Because our weekly meetings are too infrequent for everyone to stay up to date with new information and on the same page.

In the first problem, the team not finishing strong was a symptom of a much bigger issue – namely, the team's culture. In the second problem, the project manager was not holding productive meetings, and key people were not receiving critical information. In both cases, the five-why method helped the leader sift through the symptoms to identify the root or cause, of the problem.

Now that you have identified the root cause of the problem with your inner circle, you can reach out to your PBA for potential solutions. Get the most out of your mentors by having a specific question to present to them. Try to use them for problem-solving, not problem identification. Take notes so that you can reference them later, and let them know how much it means to you. They are, after all, volunteering their time to make you and your organization better.

After discovering possible solutions with your PBA, you can discuss the process with your expanding circle. Now, you can provide a stimulating conversation that will help them improve. You are not selling them. You are sharing with them. You are creating value in those relationships, which will make them stronger and create longer- lasting connections.

Accept Feedback

It is important to remember that the more honest and vulnerable you are, the more well rounded and applicable the advice will be. The value is not convincing your PBA that you are right, but rather to facilitate and open up a dialogue. Lay it all on the table and expect them to do the same. Yes, it will sometimes sting a bit when people are honest with you. There is nothing wrong with that, as long as you can move past it. Elite people don't want to be right. They want to be better. Accept your feedback with humility and respect.

These relationships take time to nurture. If you respond poorly, then they will no longer offer constructive criticism. You have to humble yourself, and it's going to sting a bit, or at least it should. Don't forget that these people are offering you an excellent service and you should treat them with the utmost respect. There is indeed a fine line between confidence and arrogance. Do you remember the difference? Confidence involves knowing that you are up to any task; arrogance is thinking that you are above it. Be confident in your process and accept that you have selected these people because they are at polar opposites of multiple spectrums. Simply receive, reflect, and maintain a thankful heart.

Start Building

If you are not actively trying to expand your network by making relationships built to last, then you should start now. It takes a proactive approach to surround yourself with elite people. Remember that the best way to demonstrate your value is to be yourself. Try to connect with people on a personal level. Use their first name often so that they know you care. Ask about family and listen. Spend time with these people without asking for anything. Your expanding circle is not a sales call, although people do tend to do business with people that they like and trust. Play the long game by being authentic and showing people that they matter to you.

Choose a PBA that has diverse opinions, skill sets, professional backgrounds, and even worldviews. There are things that we know, things that we don't know, and things that we don't even know that we don't know yet. The last category is the dangerous one – the enemies that you are not even aware of. Choosing a diverse and experienced PBA will illuminate that column and will save you time, money, and heartache, guaranteed.

Finally, choose an inner circle of people who know you well, have known you for a long time, and believe in you. Not everyone will get you or believe in you. Those people are the ice cubes that will steal the heat from your coffee. Choose people that you want to rub off onto you, because they will. The longer you have known them, the more comfortable you will be opening up to them about the real issues in your life. With these three circles, you will make better decisions, grow as a person, and gain confidence because you have surrounded yourself with the right people.

Becoming Elite!

1. Stop selling and start connecting. Expand your circle by building genuine relationships.
2. Remember that being authentic is the pathway to longevity. Play the long game.
3. Diversify your PBA. Find people who will disagree with you and each other.
4. Use your inner circle to help you with the five whys to see through symptoms and identify problems.
5. Use your PBA for their experience in solving problems, not for their ability to identify problems.
6. Be sure to give as much as you receive. Always look for ways to pay it forward.

CHAPTER

8

Pursue Mentorship

N ow that we have our expanding circle, our PBA, and our inner circle, let's explore the fourth kind of relationship that you can add to your life – namely, the mentor. Learning new lessons always costs us something. It can cost time, money, relationships, and even our jobs. In business school, they would call this learning curve cost. Learning lessons the hard way can be avoided by adding a mentor to your life. If you learn from someone who has more experience than you, it will save you severe pain. People who are elite learn from others' mistakes, so they don't make the same mistakes themselves. They also look at other people's achievements and learn from those as well. A mentor can help in both cases. Of course in my case, it caused me a little bit of pain as well.

Mistakes Were Made

When I was a new guy, meaning that I had made it through SEAL training but had zero experience, I showed up to the SEAL team pretty cocky. All of us new guys were. Coming off one of the most significant accomplishments of our young lives was a high point. The truth, however, was that we were all new guys and didn't know anything yet. The only thing we had accomplished at that point was training. Overconfidence combined with inexperience leads to costly mistakes. Fortunately, right when I needed it most, I found someone who would affect me.

It was a typical day at work. We would muster at 9 a.m. for a meeting, break for a workout, and begin prepping the SEAL delivery vehicle (SDV). The SDV is a small submarine that we were going to be training with later that night after the sun went down. We would have all day to prep the equipment necessary, which was no small task. I had decided to ride my motorcycle to work that day and got into a disagreement with the guy at the gate about whether I needed a reflector vest to ride a motorcycle on a Navy base. This exchange made me late for my platoon's morning meeting.

I was late walking in the door, but only by about two minutes. Jim Boa, my platoon chief, made a comment that went something like, "nice of you to join us this morning," as I found a chair next to the rest of my platoon who had already gathered and were waiting on a full headcount to begin. An important note here is that a new guy in a SEAL platoon is expected to show up to all meetings 15 minutes early. A common saying is, "if you're not early, you're late." In response to my two minutes of tardiness, my platoon chief Jim asked me to stay behind after he ended the meeting.

His face was not overly stern and did not show even an ounce of anger. He spoke plainly and with little inflection in his voice. "It's obviously not that big of a deal, but being late is probably not the best way to start the day," he said with a slight chuckle and dismissive hand gestures. "No drama, but go ahead and fill a rucksack (military speak for backpack) with 50 pounds of weight and run up the para-loft tower one time for every guy in the platoon. Then we're even." I thought he was joking at first, considering the para-loft tower was five stories high and we had 20 guys in our platoon. It seemed a little bit harsh for a two-minute infraction. Still, I figured it might be a test, so I would play the game.

Learning Curve Cost

I went downstairs and filled up my rucksack with 50 pounds. As I threw it on my back, ready to walk to the tower, I heard Jim's voice, who had apparently followed me down. "You can't do it now, brother, that would be in place of your workout and wouldn't even be a punishment. You have to do it after work." Now, I knew that he was probably just giving me a hard time. It had seemed like a joke when he told me, and he apparently wasn't even angry. I dropped the bag, and we went and worked out together for an hour or so before beginning our gear prep for a night dive. For the rest of the day Jim never brought up my morning infraction, it seemed that I was in the clear.

Night fell, and we splashed the SDV into the water. It was a long dive, so we didn't finish until well after midnight. When a dive is over, the work is not. We always clean up the team gear first, then your swim buddy's gear, then, at the end of it all, you take care of your gear. An hour or so later I was rinsing out my wetsuit, dive fins, and mask when Jim walked up and said, "don't forget the rucksack, brother." My heart sank with the realization that a punishment that clearly did not fit the crime was still looming in my painful future.

I was furious. Despite my anger, I knew better than to show weakness on my face or express anything other than good humor to my platoon mates, who would have undoubtedly been brutal had they smelled blood. Instead of voicing my opinion, I grabbed my rucksack and began the walk of shame to the para-loft tower.

As I walked closer, I could see that Jim was standing at the door of the tower. The sight fueled my anger at first. Did he not trust that I would do it? Did he bring a scale to weigh my bag and make sure that I wasn't cheating? As I got closer, I noticed that something was lying at Jim's side, but it was not a scale; it was a rucksack.

Upon my approach, he picked it up and threw it on his back. He told me that my failures are his failures and that he is the leader of the platoon and ultimately responsible for my actions. My pain would be his pain. That was all that he said, nothing more. He turned and ran up the first flight of stairs, and

I followed. We ran every flight of stairs together that night. Five stories, 20 times, with 50 pounds on our backs after a 14-hour workday.

He never gave me a hard time or said anything more about it during those painful hours. In fact, we found ourselves laughing. We talked about God, family, the mission, and whatever else popped into our heads. I knew at that moment that I could trust this man. I knew that he cared enough to invest in me and show me a better way. Jim cared enough to teach, and I was happy to learn.

Value of a Mentor

Throughout my tenure with that platoon, I would look to Jim as a guide. When we started a new block of training, I would look at his gear and make sure that mine looked exactly like his. I figured he'd learned a thing or two in his seven deployments and that I could save a lot of time, and possibly pain if I modeled my gear, equipment, rucksack, weapon system, and even daily routine after him. I learned about raising children, having faith, and being a husband from our conversations. Eventually, on deployment, we would pray together before going out the door on a high level mission. Not too long after that, we stood side by side as they pinned Bronze Stars on our chests at an award ceremony.

I was young, talented, overconfident, and in desperate need of a mentor. When I found one and saw that value, I held on for dear life. I became a better operator for the experience, but I also became a better man. Perhaps more importantly, I learned quite a bit about how to lead a collection of high-octane individuals. One essential trick of the trade for elite individuals is to find solid mentorship. Avoid the learning curve cost associated with operating at a high level by sticking close to someone who has faced the issues you are about to face and ultimately overcome. Listen, learn, and take notes. I had been successful, but talent would only take me so far. I was charging full steam ahead, but my course needed some correction.

Course Correction

To put it in another way, I was navigating my proverbial ship in the right general direction but was off by a degree or two. I'll take a moment to explain that for anyone who has not experienced navigation by compass. When you want to travel somewhere, say in a boat without a GPS, you'll need to know where you currently are, where you want to be, and the bearing that will get you there. You need all three pieces of information for accurate navigation on the water without any landmarks. If you need to steer my ship on a bearing of 270 for 100 meters, then you would position the ship to face that bearing and start moving. If you're only traveling 100 meters, and you accidentally travel on a bearing of 272, then you may still get where you are going. Sure you were slightly off course, but you weren't traveling very far. If you travel for 1,000 meters that two-degree difference adds up to much more deviation. The deviation in your course has left you in a different location than you initially set out to for. If you intend to land on the center of an island but have allowed two degrees of deviation in your navigation, then you might hit the southern tip by accident. If the island is small enough, then you may miss it all together.

Now imagine that you are leaving Los Angeles, California and you shoot a bearing that should land you in Hawaii. Without GPS or landmarks, you shoot a bearing and begin traveling. At times you may lose focus and look away. Maybe the wind blows, and you lose the wheel for a moment. Whatever the reason, all this distraction, external influence, and human error allows for about two degrees of deviation. Do you think you would get to Hawaii? The answer is no. You have been off course for far too long to get back to your intended destination without changing your course.

Life without a mentor is like navigating without course corrections. You will miss the mark. If you are starting a new career, and you don't have a mentor, you will waste valuable time listening to peers who do not necessarily have the same aspirations as you do. If you are starting a diet, you may choose foods that you think are healthy based on the products marketing campaign, regardless of whether or not it is healthy. Apply this logic to raising kids, communicating with your spouse, choosing a career, or accepting a leadership position. Can you afford to miss the mark or learn those lessons the hard way? Not if your dream is to become elite.

The cost savings that you will get from having a mentor who can offer course corrections along the way is substantial. When you are trying something new, there will be a direct cost associated with your inexperience. The longer you are exposed to the environment the lower that cost will become. Adding a mentor to your life will lower that cost dramatically as depicted in Figure 8.1. The sooner you develop this kind of relationship the sooner you will begin experiencing the savings.

Choosing a Mentor

Choosing a mentor can be hard, but here are a couple of tips on who to look for. Trust is the first factor that you will need to build a lasting relationship. You must trust your mentor to be without a conflict of interests and to be confidential. You must be able to talk to this person about the things you are the least

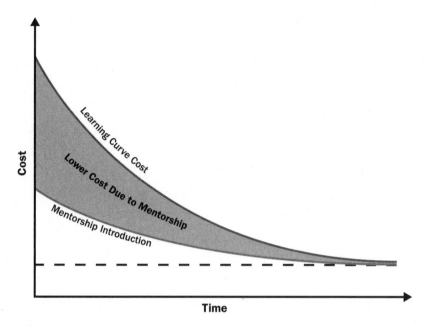

FIGURE 8.1 Learning Curve Cost

proud of with yourself. It is hard to admit you are wrong, and if you will be tempted to put a spin of the story if you think the person may use the information against you.

You must also trust their expertise. A mentor who is more experienced than you will have the best advice and be able to provide the most positive effect. Learning from those who have experience, have dealt with similar problems, and have worked in related industries will have the most value. Yes, industries change over time. Your job is to synthesize the information that you learn from them with your changing context.

Finally, look for a mentor who isn't afraid of the hard conversations. Your mentor's ability to push you and challenge you will cause you to be uncomfortable. There will be growing pains but remember, if you're not uncomfortable, they're not doing their jobs.

Let Your Mentor Know

Does the story about my platoon chief Jim make you think about someone who cared enough to invest his or her life in you? Can you remember a time when you were in need of a serious course correction that needed attention? Consider what that may have cost you, in the long run, had you not found a mentor? I want to officially challenge you to identify the people who have taken part in making you who you are today. Then reach out to them, regardless of how long it has been. Give them a call and thank them. Also, tell them exactly what they did that helped you so much so that they know their efforts were effective and appreciated. It will do more than make your mentor feel good. It will provide him with valuable feedback and motivation to continue mentoring others to become elite.

Elite Mentors Create Elite Mentors

In the SEAL teams, we believe that it is everyone's responsibility to lead. Finding a mentor and knowing how to ask and implement his or her advice is critical. It is also important to pay it forward. Regardless of your age, your rank, or your title, it is your responsibility to mentor others who will stand to gain from your level of experience. You are never too young. Believe me. I watched my seven-year-old daughter mentor my four-year-old son in the swimming pool, and I was proud as a parent.

I have referenced our SEAL ethos several times in this book. A portion of it talks about the concept of leadership at every level: "We expect to lead and be led. In the absence of orders, I will take charge, lead my teammates and accomplish the mission. I lead by example in all situations." Our ethos was created for the new guy, the platoon chief, and the veteran.

We believe that everyone shares the responsibility to lead and to mentor. At any given point in his career, a Navy SEAL has a mentor and is also a mentor to others simultaneously. It is your responsibility as an aspiring individual who desires to operate at the elite level to pull others under your wing.

How to Mentor Others

The role of a mentor is to observe who the person is, taking account of the person's personality type, as well as his or her strengths and weaknesses. The mentor must also consider where that person wants to be and what may be holding the individual back. Helping the person shed light on his or her personal or professional areas for improvement is a responsibility of the mentor. It means having the hard conversations because that creates the friction necessary for growth. It can be hard to tell someone that you care about when they are off course, but that's ok. We have all needed a course correction in our lives. If you are an experienced member of the team, a coach, or even a junior person who has identified the need, then it is your obligation to let them know and help them devise a plan to get back on course. After all, their faults are your faults, and their successes are your successes.

The ancient proverb says, "As iron sharpens iron, so one person sharpens another." It takes friction to sharpen the blade. Elite teams have powerful mentors who allow the friction of discourse when the blade is dull, who take ownership of their actions and the actions of their teammates. They lead by the example they set and the words that back it up. They share in the successes of the people around them. They initiate the hard conversations and respect others for having hard conversations with them. If you see that someone needs a course correction, then provide it with gentleness and humility. Telling people what they are doing right as well as providing positive reinforcement is powerful and can soften the blow of constructive criticism. Step up to the plate and invest in your teammates. After all, you are all in the same boat.

Becoming Elite!

1. Take time to think about the lessons that you have had to learn the hard way and what those lessons cost you.
2. Think about a person who has more experience than you and who believes in your ability. Ask them to mentor you. You will not know how they feel until you ask.
3. Consider your reasons for becoming a mentor and remember that sharing in someone else's success is one of the most rewarding things that you can do.
4. Practice having hard conversations. Be gentle but direct. Never leave out the positive, because it will soften the blow.
5. Reach out to your mentor and tell them thank you. He or she deserves it.

Continually Improve Your Situation

The goal of the decisions that you make should be to improve your current situation as much as possible. That's an obvious statement if I am choosing what to eat for dinner, but most decisions are a bit grayer. For instance, after my back surgery, I took pain medication for a few weeks. I'm glad that we live in a time that medications are available for intense pain. Less than a month after my surgery I decided to get off painkillers despite the doctor telling me that he would give me enough for two additional months if I wanted them. I chose to avoid chemical addiction because turning one problem into two seemed like a bad idea. Taking pain meds would make me feel better, but my situation would not have improved at all were I to become addicted to opioids.

Sometimes these decisions are obvious, but sometimes it is hard to see which choice will have the optimal outcome. Other times we don't have many options available to us. This is a story about having to choose between horrible and terrible. Now that you know my mentor and platoon chief Jim, I want to share a story about when I had to make a decision that would determine his fate.

The SEAL Delivery Vehicle

In the final weeks of BUD/S, students eagerly await orders to their first SEAL team. The BUD/S student receives his orders when he has been away from his family for a month of training. That happens off the coast of Southern California.

I would imagine that they do this so that no one can hear the screams of the unfortunate young men who get orders to what is known as the SDV team. SDV stands for SEAL delivery vehicle, which is a miniature submarine. Its purpose is to transport a small team of operators underwater, and to a selected point on a beach completely undetected. The SDV is a method of transportation that was developed for the most austere of environments and is exceptionally dangerous to conduct.

I know everything that you just read sounds pretty awesome but I assure you, it is better imagined than experienced. Aspiring students graduating from BUD/S may shed the proverbial tear when they receive their orders because they have learned a few simple truths by that point. The first is that cold water sucks. Cold water for extended durations is comically bad, and after seven months of hypothermic conditions in training, finding out that you will be diving for the next five years of your life is like getting kicked in the sweet spot by a steel-toed boot.

The second thing that every young BUD/S student knows is that the better you look in pictures, wearing all the gear that they wear in the movies and video games, the more miserable you actually are. You can't feel the weight of a thing when looking at a picture. Those viral photos you see on the internet of a SEAL emerging from the water in a wetsuit with a rifle, dive apparatus, and many other cool-looking gadgets make no mention of the 70-pound cost of looking that "cool." The moral of the story is that spending five to six hours on dive status in freezing water in a submersible that is continuously trying to kill you is not the best life choice. For the young student on the verge of being a new guy, the decision is not theirs to make. Those orders are provided by the Navy, and the needs of the Navy outweigh the needs of the individual.

A Frogman Story

To keep this story brief, I'll get right to the action. I became a pilot of the mini-submarine. I remembered Dr. Martin Luther King saying, "If a man is called to be a street sweeper, he should sweep streets even as a Michelangelo painted, or Beethoven composed music or Shakespeare wrote poetry. He should sweep streets so well that all the hosts of heaven and earth will pause to say, 'Here lived a great street sweeper who did his job well.'" Admittedly, it was not what I had joined the Navy to do, but I became the best pilot I could be. At the time there were only a few primary pilots of this craft in the United States. It was specialized, extremely challenging, and in the end, a little fun.

Our platoon had been granted an opportunity to go somewhere cool, doing something neat, for a reason that was worth it. We were training to do something that is still highly classified, so that is the most you'll get out of me on the matter. What I can tell you is how a training accident put my four-man fire team in the worst danger any of us had ever faced.

My job was to make the SDV the same weight as the water around me at around 30 feet of seawater. When the ratio was right, it would allow me to bring the submersible to a complete stop without sinking or rising to the surface. I accomplished this by changing the ratio of water (weight) and air (buoyancy) on the tanks inside the SDV to equal the pressure of the water column around me. What works at 30 feet of seawater will not work at 60 feet because there is much more pressure the deeper you go. In fact, what works at 30 feet will cause you to sink like a rock at 60 feet.

I was a good pilot, and when I came to a stop at 30 feet, the SDV stuck in the water column like Velcro. What I didn't know is that we were brushing alongside an anchor line that was dug in under 300 feet of seawater. It scraped across the side of the sub until it came into contact with our one and only propeller. The line wrapped around the propeller and quickly rendered it useless. Remember my chief Jim? Well, he was one of the four in my fire team on this mission. He grabbed his swim buddy, and they went outside the SDV doors and to the rear to see if they could get the line off of our propeller so that we could continue the mission.

They were able to do this because we were not in a traditional submarine that you see in the movies, which is pressurized like an airplane and in which the human body can survive at great heights or great depths. The SDV requires that every individual is wearing a dive rig, just as if he was diving in the clear, warm waters of Cancun. There is a thin door that separates us from the outside, and all the personnel inside are fully submerged in water, so we were at the mercy of what our bodies could handle as divers.

Now, if you've ever been diving, you had to learn that people cannot go very deep without serious repercussions. There are ways to mix various kinds of gasses to extend what the body can withstand before being seriously injured, but sadly, we were not diving with mixed gas. We were on the same air that we breathe on the surface every day meaning that the maximum depth that we were allowed to dive to was 130 feet, and only for a moment before returning to the surface. Anything more than that and the body is in serious jeopardy. For that reason, I became quickly alarmed as I saw our depth begin to decline rapidly.

We dropped to a depth of 60 feet within minutes. Although this doesn't sound extreme, it did mean that the submersible now weighed considerably more and we would continue to drop deeper. My chief and mentor Jim and his swim buddy were still outside, trying to get the propeller untied. We were able to communicate as long as one of them was looking in our direction. I peeked out the door, and Jim gave me an okay sign with his hand, so I knew they were doing just fine. I noticed that our depth gauge now said 80 feet and I came to one of the most frightening realizations of my life. We were anchored to the ocean floor and there was a three-Knott current. As the current was pushing us, and the anchor chain held, the chain would rotate down current until eventually it would lay flat at the bottom, and we would go with it. We were already heavy and sinking; the current pushing against us would only speed our descent.

Under Pressure

Let me back up here and explain something about dive physics for a moment. You must understand the science behind it if you are going to appreciate the events that followed. When we are standing on the beach at sea level, we are under what is known as one atmosphere. This is an actual unit of measurement. The space above the earth's surface actually has weight. We don't feel it because our bodies are designed to exist within that weight. Underwater, however, this changes. In fact, when I dive down to 33 feet of seawater, I am under an additional atmosphere. That's right, the weight of only 33 feet of seawater is equal to the weight of our earth's atmosphere. When the diver descends to 66 feet, that diver is under three atmospheres of pressure. The added pressure is why you cannot dive very deep for very long.

As those of you who dive know, the most dangerous thing that you can do underwater is return to the surface. The rule in diving is that you cannot ascend faster than your smallest bubble. If you go faster than that, you will be placing too much pressure on your lungs.

Here is an example. If I take a balloon and blow it up on the surface of the water, then dive that balloon down to 33 feet sea water, the balloon looks as though it is deflated, and no longer holds air. But this is not the case. In fact, the pressure of the additional atmosphere has squeezed the air inside the balloon down to practically nothing. If the diver then brings that balloon from 33 feet and back to the surface, the balloon looks as if it is filling back up and it returns to its original size upon reaching the surface.

However, if I take a balloon to 33 feet of seawater and blow it up at depth, I cannot take the balloon to the surface. The gas will expand as the balloon rises and the balloon will pop well before reaching the surface. For this reason, when a diver takes a breath at 33 feet of seawater and then ascends, the gas within his lungs will expand. When pressure on the inside of the lung becomes greater than the pressure on the outside of the lung, it can pop like a balloon. If any gas enters the arterial circulation, then it will cause an embolism. The medical term for this is an arterial gas embolism, and it is often fatal. In short, a diver can't dive deeper than 130 feet on compressed air and cannot ascend faster than his slowest bubble, or about one foot per two seconds, or 30 feet per minute.

Die Fast or Slow

Now that you know what you know, you can imagine my surprise when in the time it took you to read that last paragraph we had sunk to 140 feet of seawater. What's worse is that the air has a narcosis effect under that much pressure and it made all four of us feel as if we were completely drunk. We were moments from death, but I honestly could not stop laughing. The right thing to do at that point was to bail out of the SDV and begin swimming to the surface. Although bailing on a multimillion-dollar piece of equipment was less than ideal, it was better than dying, and we were seconds away from death.

I looked outside at my chief again and saw him making what seemed like a joke to his dive buddy. I'll be honest. Of all the ways a person can die, diving narcosis, otherwise known as the "martini effect" is not that bad. It is, however, nearly impossible to remember why you should be afraid. I came back into the submersible and saw my copilot pointing at one of the valves over our heads. I had been unable to tell the divers who were outside to bail out or get back in. I could not use the propeller to power out either because it would chop them to bits.

My only solution was to blow all the water (weight) out of the submersible and turn it into a buoy. If the air inside the SDV made us light enough, then maybe we would begin to rise. The problem was that it would cause us to rise way too quickly. If I were to take the balloon we were discussing earlier down to 140 feet, fill it up with air, and let go. It would rocket to the surface in seconds. If the submersible did the same, we would all surely die from an embolism. I was suffering from the martini effect like everyone else, but I remember asking myself one question:

Is it better to die fast or slow?

Maximize Your Upside, Minimize Your Downside

I knew that if I did nothing, we would all die. The only option that I had available wasn't much better. We might still die, but it would at least delay our death for a little while. Although there wasn't a right decision to be made, I could still choose between terrible and bad. The better choice is often the one that maximizies your upside – what you stand to gain – and minimizes your downside – what there is to lose. In one single moment, I reached for the valve and released all the weight in the submersible. I then grabbed another valve and flooded the tanks with air.

Our descent slowed quickly but did not stop. I watched with a mix of dread and martini-infused comedy while my depth gauge read 150 feet, then 155 feet then it slowed such that time began to stand still. The deepest depth that I saw on the gauge was 164 before we stopped for just a moment. Then the depth gauge read 160, 155, 150, 130. The pendulum had swung the other way, and we began to put stress on the chain that had been pulling us deeper

We slowed for a moment, suspended in the water column when I heard the loud sound of the anchor chain snap. Immediately after hearing the sound, the SDV shot like a rocket to the surface. I still did not know if my chief and his swim buddy had returned to the submersible. What I did know is that we were about to take one hell of a ride. My door was still open from when I was trying to communicate with Jim, but the water was flowing past it so violently that I had to shift my weight to the center of the SDV to avoid being sucked out into the blue abyss.

Through the door, the turbulence of water flowing past us looked like a movie from outer space, when a spacecraft is reentering the earth's atmosphere and appears to be burning up. Never in my life have I been more scared than I was in that moment.

The proper ascent rate to avoid injuring the lungs from that depth should have taken well over five minutes. We shot to the surface in 17 seconds. I felt the gas in my lungs expanding so rapidly that I blew out as hard as I could all the way up. When the SDV reached the surface, we shot out of the water like the Dallas in the movie, *Hunt for Red October.*

Once on the surface, my copilot and I exited the SDV and went to the rear to find our other two members of the fire team. They had noticed our change in direction and jumped back into the SDV before we gained speed. We found ourselves at another decision point. Knowing that some of us were about to show signs of embolism, we decided to connect ourselves to each other with carabiners. This way, if one of us went unconscious, the body would be easy to recover, and we could give them a fighting chance. We improved our situation in whatever way we could by minimizing our downside. Our support staff made their way to us in boats and rushed us to a dive chamber for emergency treatment.

When we were in the support boat, Jim told us that his arm had gone numb. Recognizing this as decompression sickness, our medical staff rushed Jim into the dive chamber for immediate treatment. The rest of us, miraculously, did not show any signs of medical issues while we waited to find out what would become of our chief. Jim was in the treatment chamber for over five hours. The dive chamber did its job, and Jim survived.

It's quite odd that we all lived. In fact, everyone said that there was no excuse for us to be alive. We were all wearing dive computers on our wrists that logged our entire adventure so I can assure you that the numbers that I've shared with you are accurate. Our leadership mailed our dive computers to the experimental dive unit for further study. The experts at that unit did not have answers. Apparently, the laws of physics can be bent a little from time to time.

Ownership

As happy as I was that we had all survived and that we had saved the SDV from the bottom of the ocean, I had been in the Navy for long enough to know what was about to happen. When something goes wrong in the Navy, there is always an investigation. Since the computers captured the entire dive, the truth was out there.

For the two days following the event, we were all interviewed separately so that our leadership could decide who was at fault for the incident. Since I was the pilot, all eyes were on me. I honestly didn't know what they would decide. Was I the cause of the anchor chain wrapping around our propeller or was it a fluke? Should we have bailed out much earlier, grabbed the two men who were trying to get the propeller unstuck, and swam to the surface? Should I have blown the weight out of the boat earlier? Not at all?

The only thing that I knew is that the future of my career and my reputation rested on people who were not down there with me. They did not feel the fear or the weight of the decision-making process, but it did not matter. Either way, I would have to live with their decision, and it was entirely out of my control. For two days I waited to hear the verdict. Was I the reason that my three closest friends almost died, or had I saved our lives?

That's the funny part. The truth did not matter half as much as the verdict. The story would outlive the experience itself. It is in these moments that we must own our actions. I was responsible even though I didn't know if I should have felt pride or shame. After reviewing the data and testimonies of the individuals, they had made their decision. Our SEAL team's leadership called me into the office, and they told me that they were proud of the way we handled it. They said that had I not blown the weight out of the boat when I did we would have been dead in moments. They also recognized that they would not have to recover a multimillion SDV from the ocean floor. Only then, did I indeed feel safe again. It was over.

Lessons Learned

The odds were that if I took action, we would probably die, but if I took no action, we would certainly die, and much sooner. The purpose of my decision was to buy us time, which was an improvement, as we did not have much time left. A good choice will improve your situation.

Once on the surface, we decided to connect ourselves to each other in case one of us went unconscious or died. This decision, however grim, minimized our downside and maximized our potential upside. A risky decision is one that maximizes your upside and minimizes your downside. You can mitigate that risk by removing the worst possible outcome as an option. A bad choice is one that minimizes your upside and maximizes your downside. You must weigh what you stand to lose against what you stand to gain if you are going to make decisions that continually improve your situation.

Becoming Elite!

1. What decision are you currently facing? What is the best possible outcome and the worst possible outcome?
2. What can you do to maximize the upside while minimizing the potential downside?
3. When you cannot control the situation, consider what you can control within the situation.
4. When the dust settles, take ownership of your actions.

Make Decisions That Produce Good Results

Simply knowing that something exists and that it works has great value. You may not be able to explain how gravity works on a whiteboard but you trust the fact that it exists, which may be enough to keep you from jumping off the Grand Canyon. In the same way, you may not know how the engine in your car works but you know how to fill it with gas, get an oil change, and get to work on time.

Although knowing something is necessary is valuable, elite people will understand how it works and this will provide them a significant advantage. The person who knows how to change his or her own oil will save money. The person who can feel the car popping and locking will begin to diagnose the problem, first checking for fouled spark plugs, clogged fuel lines, and so on. By staying ahead of the problem, the car will likely stay in better shape for longer. Similarly, if someone understands gravitation pull but also knows how moving quickly with wings that throw the air down to the ground generating the force called lift, that person can literally take flight, seemingly defying gravity.

This is true for decision-making as well. We all know how to make decisions but we're not necessarily conscious of how we are doing it. We may not understand how others are making better decisions than we are and we may not know how some people tend to be flexible and can shift strategies effectively and quickly.

The truth is, once we understand the process that our brain is using, we can jump in the driver's seat. We can learn how to train more effectively, and know when it is right to stick with a strategy and when it is right to pivot. The world stops happening to *us* and we begin happening to the *world*.

OODA Loop

The OODA loop (observe, orient, decide, and act) is a decision-making structure developed by John R. Boyd, an Air Force colonel and military strategist. Boyd believed that in or order to maintain a competitive advantage, one must embrace adaptation, not as a reaction, but as continual action over time. The OODA loop serves to connect the decision-maker with the environment, providing him or her the ability to assess and adapt to a rapidly changing context (see Figure 10.1).

First, we *observe* the environment around us and gather information. Raw data is collected to use later in the process. Next, we *orient* ourselves to that environment by synthesizing the data into multiple working theories. We explore the effects of every available option. Then we *decide* what we determine the best course of action and commit. Finally, we *act* on that decision swiftly to best capitalize on the moment.

We repeat the loop over and over again. The effects of that loop will determine whether the decision maker can stick with the current strategy, or if adjustments are required. Later, we will discuss when it is time to shift your loop, but first, we will

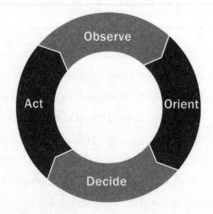

FIGURE 10.1 OODA Loop.

discuss each phase individually. I will use an example to help us visualize the process from the perspective of two mixed-martial-arts fighters.

Loop versus Loop

I want you to imagine that two elite fighters are coming up with a game plan for how they intend to fight each other. One of the fighters is short but built with muscle and is powerful. The other is tall and lanky. The taller fighter will observe that he cannot match the power of his smaller opponent but can take that power away entirely if he can keep the smaller fighter outside, meaning that the shorter fighter with a shorter reach will be unable to even throw a punch, let alone land one.

The shorter, more powerful fighter has observed that he will be unable to land a punch unless he can get inside the taller fighter's defense. He may have to eat a few punches from his opponent to get inside, throw a fury of punches, and then step out of harm's way.

Now that both fighters are prepared and have a game plan, it is time to fight. The taller opponent has observed that he should keep the shorter fighter out of range by using a long stiff jab. To best accomplish this strategy he must orient himself in a defensive stance, standing square to his opponent, both of his feet directly under his shoulders so that he can circle his smaller opponent and use angles that will support his jab defense.

The shorter fighter knows that his tall rival will likely try to move around him and away from him. He has elected to orient himself in an offensive stance because it will aid in his ability to use all his working options. One foot is slightly behind his shoulders, and the other is in front of him. His aggressive stance will prevent him from moving side to side but will allow him to pounce forward to close the distance on his opponent quickly. This orientation will allow him to use slight head movements to avoid the taller fighters jab before stepping forward quickly, throwing a combo, then stepping to the side and away before the taller fighter can counter.

The shorter fighter then decides it is time to move in for the kill. He steps forward in hopes that his head movement will cause the taller fighter's punches to glance off his head instead of impacting him squarely. Simultaneously, the tall fighter sees his opponent moving closer and decides to act immediately by throwing a left jab. As the shorter fighter planned, the jab glances away from his face and leaves him unfazed. His loop is still intact. He decides to continue inside the taller fighter's reach. The taller fighter sees that his jab will be less effective at a shorter distance and quickly acts by throwing a straight right, his power punch, to the face of the short fighter. The straight right is a powerful strike and connects with the shorter fighter's forehead.

The short fighter is stunned. Both opponents begin their loops again. The taller fighter observes that his loop was successful. He is free to maintain his strategy. The short fighter, however, observes that he cannot take another strike like that to the face. He is unable to act on his initial plan but can continue working through the phases of the loop. He must orient himself differently based on his new observation.

When to Pivot

The short fighter quickly observes that he must find a new way inside. He knows that the taller fighter is expecting him to stand up and throw punches due to his history of boxing and Muay Thai kickboxing. He observes that he could use his opponent's expectation against him in a surprise offensive move. He then orients himself in an offensive posture, the same poster that he used initially to conceal his change in strategy.

Next, he *decides* to move inside and wait for the taller fighter to throw another straight right. When he does, the shorter opponent *acts* with a level change. His hips drop low to avoid the strike as he lunges forward in a single motion to shoot in for a double leg takedown. He puts both arms behind the taller fighter's thighs as he drives forward with his hips to take the tall fighter off of his balance and onto his back on the floor. Now, both fighters need to abandon their previous loops and start all over again with *observation*.

You have used this same loop, maybe even without knowing it, multiple times. Think of the last time that you were driving down the road, and the person in front of you slammed on the breaks. I'm sure that before you even had time to consider the implications of a collision consciously, you were able to react in a way that kept you from harm's way. The loop was there, but it happened so quickly that your brain responded on full auto. You *observed* the red lights on the car in front of you and the speed change that would lead to a collision unless you took immediate action. Your brain signaled your body to *orient* itself to the situation. Your right foot went to the brake pedal. You grabbed the steering wheel with both hands. Maybe you even put your arm across the chest of the person sitting next to you. Then you *decided* that immediate action was necessary while checking the rear view mirror for someone riding your tail. Then you took *action*, hit the brake, and avoided an accident.

It is important to consider that the more time you spent behind the wheel of a vehicle before being in that situation likely determined how quickly your brain could step into the loop, the quality of that loop, as well as assessing your available options. The take-away is this: experience, exposure, specific training, and visualization will dramatically improve the quality of your loop and will quicken the speed at which you can move through the phases of the loop.

Train How You Fight

Any of the veterans or police officers reading this book will understand the value of a transition drill. When a team of operators is clearing a house from room to room, they will ideally be doing it with a rifle. If that operator enters a room and sees a threat, he may pull the trigger. Pretty simple, but what happens if the gun does not fire? If there is a malfunction with the rifle, the operator will not have time to fix the problem before the threat begins to shoot back. For this reason, the operator will immediately transition to his pistol to finish off the threat before getting his primary rifle back up and running.

Time is precious in those seconds, so it is faster and more efficient to drop the rifle and pull your pistol then it is to try and fix the problem with the rifle. For this reason, we attach weapon slings to the rifle. We can let go of the rifle, and it hangs freely in front of us. The only way to make sure that you will make that decision under the stress of a life-threatening situation is to practice it time and time again in training.

You may have heard the statement that practice makes perfect. This statement is only half true though. In fact, perfect practice makes perfect. We have a saying in the SEAL teams: train how you fight. Train precisely the way that you will be expected to perform. If a basketball player's job is to shoot a basketball with his uniform on while exhausted in the fourth quarter, then he shouldn't take off his shirt during shoot-around because he is tired. If a project manager plans on using Powerpoint during a company meeting, then he should practice with his Powerpoint up in front of him so that his flow is natural and not forced. If a runner is running a race at altitude, then why would she train at sea level? You get the point. Practice is only useful if it adequately simulates the situation and the environment. Train how you fight.

The Speed of Your Loop

Operators will train for transition drills every time they are on a shooting range. If the rifle doesn't fire, the rifle is dropped and the pistol is pulled out to finish off the target. By training in this way over and over, the operator builds what is known as muscle memory. Meaning that the repetition of the action is so ingrained in the brain that the muscles move before the mind can even think the thought. It is a reflex action, ingrained through proper training.

Now think of the weapon transition from the viewpoint of the OODA loop. The identification of a threat and the decision to use the rifle that is already in hand and ready to fire is a loop of its own. When the weapon becomes jammed, the operator finds himself at the beginning of the loop, observing that his gun will not fire. Now he must orient himself accordingly.

Remember the fighter example. Both elite fighters were using loops against each other. The fighter who was able to begin the loop again, and move through it quicker than his opponent was the fighter who ended up on top when the fight went to the ground. It is the same with this example. The operator's gun would not fire, he had to work through the loop fast enough to avoid being shot by his enemy. The speed of the transition is directly related to the exposure that the operator has (experience) and the muscle memory that he has built into his neural pathways (training).

The Quality of Your Loop

When I left the SEAL teams and started working on a contract basis to combat zones, I had to adapt to a new way of doing things. In the teams, I had been using a SIG Sauer P226 for a decade. With my new employer I started using a Glock. I went from using a holster on my chest to using a concealed pistol carried under a shirt. These may sound like small changes, but they are not at all. If I'm using my rifle and it had a malfunction, then I must transition to my pistol quickly. If I have trained for years to go straight to my chest for my pistol as a result of muscle memory, I may not observe that I have reached for a gun that is not there until it is too late. Through proper training and repetition, we build habits that are hard to break. When the consequence for reaching for a gun that does not exist could mean death, the muscle memory needs to be retrained.

The most significant factor on the quality of your loop is preparation. Knowledge of the situation will enhance the observation phase of any decision. The quality of the orientation phase will improve if you have an appreciation for consequence.

I knew that I could reduce the learning curve cost of creating new muscle memory if I were to ask a member of my personal board of advisors for help. I flew to Philadelphia and spent a week with him because he had already changed from using a chest rig to a concealed carry. We spent an entire week shooting and running through transition drills. That week got me moving in the right direction, but it was nowhere near enough to compensate for a decade of consistently training a different way.

Shortly after, I deployed to the Middle East. Every night I would practice drawing from a concealed carry and dry fire into a mirror to improve the quality of the action. I did it every night, right before I went to bed. I did it so much, in fact, that I began dreaming about it. When you practice or visualize something before falling asleep, your brain is more likely to review it in your dreams. It is like getting free time added to your day, and I highly recommend it. Before long, working from a concealed carry became second nature. The quality of my loop had improved as well as the speed it would take me to move through all four phases.

Now that you understand how the process works in the competitive environment, you can see how the two loops of the competitors are at war. Let us discuss how you can add this structure to your life.

In Practice

Let's apply the OODA loop to a career decision. You have been excelling at work, and both your boss and your competitor have noticed that you are a rising star. Your current competitor offers you a comparable job with higher pay. Your current supervisor has offered you hope that a promotion is in your future. You have just entered the observation phase. You will gather as much raw data as you can before moving forward. You will want to learn your boss's timeline with regard to the promotion, the stability of both companies, whether relocation is required, what the retention rate is for employees at the new company, and so on.

Once you have collected the data, you will orient yourself appropriately. This phase involves developing a working theory of all your options. Think through what would happen if you went to the other company and considered all possible consequences. Consider whether telling your current supervisor about the job offer will speed up the timeline for promotion or hurt your efforts by damaging your reputation as a loyal employee. Work through all possible scenarios.

Let's say that you decide that having a conversation about the job offer with your boss is your best course of action because it is maximizing your upside while minimizing your potential downside, meaning you don't have much to lose but a lot to gain.

You act swiftly and decisively by scheduling a meeting. At the meeting, you observe that your boss did not intend to offer you a promotion quickly due to other constraints and the hope that he provided was little more than a carrot on the other end of a stick.

You have already started a new loop and are back in the observation phase. The speed of the process is much faster this time because only one variable has changed and you have already done a majority of the work. You move through the new loop quickly, you make your decision and act by finishing your negotiations with the competitor.

You started with a strategy to climb the corporate ladder and become a leader. The structure that you put into place by using the OODA loop allowed you to gather as much data as you could, consider all possible outcomes, make a decision based on the best possible outcome and then to take action quickly. The result is that you have not missed any details, had more confidence when it was time to make a decision, and were able to act before any of the variables had changed.

Becoming Elite!

1. Adding a structure to your decision-making process will allow you to make better, well thought out decision.
2. Try using simulation, repetition, and visualization to improve your performance.
3. Use the orient phase to consider all possible outcomes and various strategies
4. Train how you fight.
5. Understand that your competitors may not be using a structure in their process and you have the competitive advantage.

CHAPTER
11

Guard Your Time

Imagine with me for a second. You take 10 thousand dollars in cash out of the bank. You want to keep it in case of emergency, and you know that you will need to hide it well if you expect to still have it by the time the crisis happens. You decide to either bury it on your property in a waterproof bag, keep it concealed under your mattress, or put it in your air conditioning duct. If you have a better idea, then imagine that. With that amount of money concealed somewhere on your property, how confident would you feel about its security? How often would you check on it? Every time you have company? Every day? Ten thousand dollars is a lot of cash, after all.

We have a natural tendency to guard our money. Most of us use a balance sheet so that we can keep track of how much money is coming in and how much is going out every month. We know how much is in our savings and our retirement accounts. We know if we can afford a new car or even a new shirt. If other people feel entitled to our money, we are offended. It is *your* money, after all. No one else can say that they believe it should be theirs. You earned it and giving it away is your choice. Money doesn't come easily after all. It takes time to earn it, and you never know what is going to happen in the future. If we feel so strongly about how we get, use, and give our money, then why are we so easy to give away the one thing that we cannot get any more of. Our time.

My favorite comic book superhero was the Wolverine from *X-Men*. There was a montage at the beginning of one of his self-titled movies that shows him and his brother, Sabretooth, fighting in the Civil War, then in World War I, then in World

War II, Vietnam, and so on. Their longevity is possible because they have a rare mutation, which allows their cells to regenerate faster than they can be destroyed. Not to say that Wolverine was invincible, but he is pretty darn close. The man has unlimited time and is going to look 35 forever. If you're like me, you're a little jealous. Living forever is man's oldest quest after all.

The Wolverine might have unlimited time, but that is the sort of thing that only exists in fiction writing. The rest of us are stuck with a life that passes way too quickly when things are good and way too slowly when they are bad. They say that time heals all wounds, which is true, but it is ultimately worse than the injury itself. The wound hurts, but time is going to kill you. People are killed by time 100% of the time. We cannot buy more of it, save it up for a rainy day, or even store it in our mattress. Why then are we more concerned with who or what is taking our money than who or what is taking our time? There is an unlimited supply of money out there in the world, but your amount of time cannot be restocked and is more valuable than gold. For this reason, I would like for you to start thinking about the phrase *spend your time*. Let that word *spend* really sink in. You *are* spending it, just like you would money. And there are no returns or refunds on the expense.

Social Media

Knowing how to safeguard your time is something that everybody struggles with, even the elite of the elite. We certainly get better at it with age, but by then it is often too late. In fact, one of people's greatest regrets on their deathbeds is not guarding their time. The odds are that our generation will be much worse in this regard then generations past, due to recent technologies revolutionizing our social tendencies. A barrage of social media has consumed our lives. What started as a tool to share baby pictures turned into a critical method of communicating your business and creating brand perception. It is a necessary part of any marketing strategy because people log so many hours a day on those platforms. Of course, the marketing does not stop with our business. We also market our lifestyles regularly. It is a perpetual first date, best foot forward, approach to controlling how others perceive our lives and it is easy to become consumed.

According to Statista.com, the average time spent on social networking by internet users worldwide was 118 minutes a day in 2016. It has gone up by about 10 minutes a year for the past five years. That is a worldwide number, by the way; it is a global problem. Two hours *a day*. I wonder how much time the average father plays catch with his son. How much time a day a husband looks his wife in the eyes and has a meaningful conversation. How many minutes a day the average person spends reading or learning valuable information.

In large part, social media is somewhat mindless. We scroll through what people are up to as if to live vicariously through them while sitting on our couch. We are provided unrealistic expectations about what a happy life is by getting glimpses of the lives of others, as if one moment is enough to paint a picture of the other person's entire day.

So we get off the couch and take a picture of the sunset to post so that others think that we did something productive that day. It is a perpetual cycle of spending our time on other people, most of whom do not really care. We desire more likes as if to validate our experience. And by the way, chasing likes is like a disease. We feel a temporary kind of euphoria that involves a dopamine release when a post does well. It is the same feeling that you can achieve with a tasty dessert, a first kiss, a high-risk activity, or robbing a bank. Just kidding.

But seriously, although it is a minor and seemingly harmless thing to enjoy getting more likes on various social media platforms, it is still something that you should do in moderation. Anything in excess is harmful in the long run. I am not saying that spending your time on social media is terrible, just that elite people have learned to monitor how much time they spend so that they can achieve a healthy balance in their personal lives. No husband wants to talk to his wife while she stares at her phone. It is a sure-fire way to get your husband to disconnect with you. He will feel like you don't care or need his presence and will deal with it by tuning out. Just in case you're wondering why he's tuned out. Instead, put down your device and pick up a deck of cards. Spend time together offline, and you will find that it is time well *spent*.

In the Workplace

As I said before, I understand that there is a business component to this. There are a certain number of minutes a day that are required to run a successful brand, and there is no reasonable argument against adding social media to your business and pushing brand awareness through an organic marketing campaign. Of course, spending time looking at your accounts at work is another subject entirely. According to digitaltrends.com, the average American spends about 4.7 hours using data on their phone a day. The average American logs into their social media accounts 17 times a day. Considering the average American is only awake for 16 hours a day, those numbers are staggering. It also means that it is happening at work.

How we spend our time at work really does matter. Any entrepreneur knows how valuable time is because he or she never has enough of it. There is always another call, another spreadsheet, or another decision to make. Time spent on social media must have a purpose and must be related to the professional endeavor. The problem is that when we get bored, our work schedule can digress into staring at the clock for enough days to receive and cash a paycheck. Wash, rinse, and repeat. Often, the mundaneness of it all causes us to begin wasting time. After all, sometimes we can do what we want to do, and other times we do what we have to do. Work is something that we have to do to provide for our families and to ensure that we can enjoy the time left for ourselves.

Providing for yourself and your family is a noble quality and an excellent thing, keep it that way by not allowing it to become an excuse to steal your employer's time and money. Spending extra time in the bathroom or logging into your social media accounts when you have been tasked to do something else is dishonest. You are hurting the company and the margin that ultimately results in your paycheck. You are also destroying the possibility of being noticed and considered for a promotion, which will result in more money. And if money is the only reason that you are working in the first place, that factor should matter a great deal.

Find Your Why

I would argue, however, that if your only incentive to go to work is to earn money, then you are missing out. One of the essential elements of a happy and fulfilled life is the purpose that we have for doing the things that we do. As a father, I know that every ounce of time spent playing with or educating my children is time that I will never regret and will ultimately make them better citizens. Children have provided me a greater depth to my sense of purpose in life. As a Navy SEAL, I knew that what

I was doing mattered to the global environment and my country. I had a professional purpose that was a far greater incentive than anything monetary. It was worth *spending* my time. If you are living your life without purpose, then you will need to get rid of the things that are sucking the life (and time) out of you and expand into the areas that will provide you a greater sense of accomplishment and add depth to the purpose in your life.

If you are not satisfied with your career, then you are essentially wasting your time. Life is more important than the number in your bank account or the nicest car that a bank will allow you to borrow for the next five years. If you get a sinking feeling every time you think about work, if you are punching a clock, and if there is no enjoyment in it, then you probably shouldn't spend a third of your life doing it. Remember, the goal is to value your time more than your money. There is never enough time, and it is going to kill you. I challenge you to be open to making a change. Part of becoming elite is finding a purpose that will reward you on a higher level than pure monetary gain.

Start with writing down purposes that excite you. The things that make you tick as a person. The kind of websites that you visit will give you some good insight into what you enjoy. Think about the causes that would give you a greater sense of purpose if you could only get involved. Then ask yourself what skill sets you would need to be part of a team whose mission is to fulfill that same purpose. Do you have any of those skills? Could they be developed? Keep in mind that the world is changing so fast that new skill sets are popping up every day.

If you want to change fields entirely, you can do a quick search on a website to see what positions will pay enough to provide for your dependents while still providing more by way of professional satisfaction. You do not have to quit your job to do this. You can easily update your resume and continue actively applying to jobs risk free. If a better opportunity comes along, then the change will be seamless, and you'll have bargaining power because of your current pay. Think about it. Even if it takes a couple of years, there is no risk and very little time spent. You will find yourself in a better position than if you were not to make those efforts to improve your situation or learn the skill sets necessary to move on to a more rewarding career.

Consider the time that President Kennedy toured the NASA space center in 1962. He walked past a man in uniform and introduced himself saying, "Hello, I'm Jack Kennedy. What are you doing?" The uniform the man was wearing was that of a janitor, and he was carrying a broom. He answered the President by saying, "I'm helping put a man on the moon." The janitor knew that he was a part of something much more significant than his job title. He was on a team that was tasked with doing the impossible which gave him pride and purpose. Even as a janitor, his time was well spent.

Listen, your time is valuable. It is also *yours*. How you spend it is your choice. There are indeed constraints that will not change; your bills, your mortgage, contractual obligations, working your way up the ladder, and your family responsibilities. But you can find a way to meet those requirements in a way that is not wasting your time. Instead of spending time on social media, spend that time searching for a career that you will find more rewarding. If you want to excel at your current career, then get off social media and get to work. You will have the competitive advantage against your peers.

Other people will often feel like they are entitled to your time as if you owe it to them. As we read earlier, you are responsible for surrounding yourself with the right people. Those people should be giving as much as they are receiving. If all they do is take your time and energy, then you should consider filling that time with something else. Find someone to mentor, someone to mentor you. You could donate your time to a good cause that helps others who actually need it. Volunteering for a cause that you believe in will fill your heart with joy and purpose. Consider spending the extra time on your spouse and children that is time worth spending.

If you get proactive about how you allocate your time, both at work and at home, you will begin to see how much of your time has been stolen by other people and obligations. You will also see an increase in personal joy, professional development, and advancement, as well an increase in productivity. After all, your time is too valuable just to give away.

Becoming Elite!

1. Don't let your social media activity define or limit you.
2. Stealing company time will hurt you professionally.
3. Who are you hurting by allowing your time to be taken?
4. How could you better assign that time to become elite?

Guard Your Mind

Having worked alongside elite people my entire career I have noticed many commonalities. One is that elite people feel responsible for controlling the information that they allow into their minds. Sometimes they need to learn more information to become subject-matter experts and other times they need to remove harmful information that could be distractions. You are responsible for the information that you allow into your mind. This is because your thoughts will eventually turn into actions and your actions will ultimately turn into habits. Make no mistake about it, you are responsible for controlling your internal environment and guarding your mind.

Hell Week

I remember it as if it were yesterday. The sun was melting into the waters of the Pacific Ocean on the horizon. As the sun's light shriveled into the black, cold waters of the sea, the heat from the day left with it. Every muscle in my body was fatigued. More than 24 hours of pure challenge was behind me now. I had carried boats over my head, been pushed to the limit with long telephone pole like logs, and ran race after race for more than a day straight.

The sun was leaving, but we would not sleep that night or the night after for that matter. In the first few weeks of BUD/S, the students must make it through the most grueling training that our military has to offer, Hell Week. In this week, we would run a total distance of nearly 200 miles, spend most of our time in borderline hypothermic conditions, and lose most of our class to either injury or their decision to quit. There would be two 2-hour naps provided on different days at the end of the week, but other than that, we were awake the entire week. It would be a mental and physical test of our resolve, the likes of which I had never come close to experiencing.

The only reprieve from the torment was the sun shining overhead throughout the long day. I knew that as long as it was high in the sky, the instructor cadre of the Naval Special Warfare Center could only punish me with physical activity. As long as the sun was out, the only pain that I would feel was in the form of lactic acid building up in my muscles. Unfortunately, that was all about to change.

In the darkness of the night, the BUDs instructors would make the entire class link arms and walk to the ocean surf until we were up to our knees before they would tell us to fall on our backs. Then we would lay on our backs, just barely able to breathe through the pounding waves. The cold of the Pacific would envelop us for what seemed like forever. Without physical activity to provide a distraction, we spent this time inside our minds. Lying in the cold water, waves smacking you in the face, turns your mind into a battlefield. The negative demon would show up from time to time and share what unpleasantries he could, and for many members of the class, his words would drive them to stand up, walk away from their classmates, and ring the bell. Ringing the bell is loud and is designed to tell the rest of the class that you are quitting.

After a time, just before members of our class became hypothermic, the instructors would pull us from the water and subject us to more log PT, boat carries, or anything else that would push us to our breaking point. Once our bodies were warmed up through activity, they would put us back in the water and drive us back to the point of hypothermia. It was what it was. Not one of us could change that, and it was going to be a long, cold night.

Not Your Average Joe

When you imagine a guy showing up for Navy SEAL training, you probably envision some actor on TV who is working on his third cycle of steroids and just got off from role-playing a futuristic, genetically mutated vigilante. TV has a way of misshaping our expectations in that way. The people casting those roles want to capture the strength of a person, both internally and externally, by showing a muscle-bound science experiment on the screen.

In reality, however, the people who often accomplish the most do not resemble their television personalities – that is to say, most of the time. When I was a young, BUD/S student on his way to becoming a Navy SEAL, I met a fellow student who blended the on-screen perception with reality. For the sake of the story, I will call this man William.

William was a remarkable story. To say that he was a keen athlete before showing up to BUD/S would be an understatement. In fact, he had won multiple world championships as a pentathlete. To his credit, he was much more than just a great performer. He was also a great guy. The members of our BUD/S class would listen to what he said, and he was a clear-cut leader in the group. His humility and willingness to mentor were evident by the fact that his door was always left open and he would encourage anyone who wanted to stop in and talk through whatever they had going on. In short, this guy was the total package. He was strong, humble, talented, and a natural leader.

I, on the other hand, was a much different story altogether. William was tall, strong jaw, and chiseled. I was short, maybe 5 feet 5 inches tall on a good day wearing Go-Go Gadget boots. I was also a little plump around the waist, having just gained my freshmen 15 in college, not six months before arriving at training.

I'm sure that when William told his family that he was going to Navy SEAL training, they all responded positively, thinking that it was the natural progression for a guy like him. My friends and family, however, may have had some very different thoughts going through their heads. One guy from church told me that he thought I would make a better dentist.

Some of the trainees were very serious, saying things like, "I'll die before I quit." I used humor as a defense mechanism and made light of everything saying things like,

"Well, tonight is going to be cold, wet, and miserable . . . but at least it will be really long!" Some of the guys appreciated my humor, but others saw it as weakness. William was what you would call a shoe-in to becoming a SEAL. I was more of a long shot regarding public perception.

Regardless of these facts, we were entering into what is considered one of the most laborious selection processes in the world, and we were going into it together, and I was delighted to have him at my side.

The Rubber Meets the Road

In the weeks leading up to Hell Week, our class experienced long days. Waking up at 4 a.m. and training until late evening, the pace was brutal. We spent most of the day wet and sandy, and we were tested in various ways. To put it in perspective, just the run to the "chow hall" where we would eat our meals amounted to six miles of running a day. In addition to this our training evolutions included eight-mile conditioning runs, obstacle course tests, two-mile ocean swims, four-mile timed beach runs, and much more.

Many of the "I'll die before I quit guys" changed their minds. The training is optional, and anyone can quit SEAL training and return to the regular Navy at any time. When the trainee realized that he did not want to subject himself to the brutality of BUD/S continually, he could ring a bell that was mounted next to the instructor office. Sometimes, on long runs or when we trained farther away from the center, they would attach a bell on the back of a truck so that it was close and available to all would be quitters. By the time we entered Hell Week, our class had already heard that bell ring many times. But it was just getting started.

The first 24 hours of Hell Week was one of the coldest times of my life. Adding to my misery, the class was divided into groups of people that were roughly the same height. Being close to the same height is vital so that when we lift boats and logs over our heads, we can all reach and participate equally. The result was that my team was made up of the shortest people in the class. We were affectionately known as the "Smurf Crew."

The Smurfs carry the same amount of weight as every other boat crew. We travel the same distance and are held to the same standard. There is no special treatment provided for our disadvantage. The result is that we lose a lot of races. With every loss came a punishment.

My team may have been small, but it was hard to get us down. We had all been small our entire lives. We were used to having to scratch tooth and nail for any ground that we would gain. It wouldn't come easily, but that didn't matter much because we had developed mindsets that made us resistant to external influences and pressures. Twenty-four hours into the week, going into Monday night, not a single Smurf had rung the bell.

William's crew was similar to ours. Most boat crews had experienced many losses, but his boat crew had rallied around him as a pillar of strength. They were hanging tough, but they were also 6 feet tall and incredibly athletic. If they didn't win a race, then they came in second and won the next one.

They were amazing performers, and the result was that they didn't have to "pay the man" as much as the Smurfs. We, on the other hand, were punished every time we failed a race, which was every single race. Their bodies were fresher, their spirits were high, and they were the clear front runners as William led down a nearly impossible road.

The only evaluation in which the Smurfs could compete was laying in the cold water. Since we would just lie down on our backs and suffer, the battle was in the mind. There are two ways to handle that kind of sustained pain. You can become claustrophobic and pray for it to end, or you can choose to sit there and embrace the suck. Smurfs are not the only group of students who are good at suffering, however. The students either have it, or they don't. Some people are afraid of being uncomfortable. Others practice it as a skill. The stronger boat crews were the ones that were very comfortable with being uncomfortable.

On Monday night, with the sun going down, we walked pace by pace into the surf zone without any idea that everything was about to change. On Monday, the Smurf Crew and I were inching closer to the water as the sun was melting into the Pacific Ocean. Our class was strong and holding together, largely due to the leadership of William, the world champion pentathlete. Unfortunately, the class was about to experience it's first dose of adversity since beginning the long week roughly 24 hours before.

Getting wet had been inevitable. As soon as our class was about knee deep in the water, the instructors told us to fall on our backs, meaning that we were emersed in the freezing water but still able to breathe. We faced the ocean as every wave crashed, and seawater ran down our noses. You can trust me when I say that the conditions were miserable. I felt it just like everyone else, but I felt something else that was greater than the pain.

I had wanted to become a SEAL since I was young. When I was in junior high, my friends from the Mount Lemmon hike had visited the Special Warfare compound. I had read every book that had ever come out about the training and seen every movie. In fact, I was overjoyed with thankfulness to be a part of it, because not many people get to. I thought about all the times when I didn't know if I would be able to get there myself. Just getting military orders to go to SEAL training was a challenge as I mentioned at the beginning of this book. I was not the most physically powerful person there by any stretch of the imagination – some had considered me a long shot – but I was overjoyed with the opportunity.

I learned then that it is impossible to feel grateful and feel self-pity at the same time. As I was lying in the cold waters of the Pacific Ocean, my focus was on being thankful, not making excuses. Instead of the negative demon complaining and telling me how miserable I should be, my mind was filled with positive thoughts. Feeling grateful excited me and guarded my mind away from how cold it was and how far I still had to go.

This story is a "tale of two cities," however. While my fellow Smurfs and I were singing songs and telling jokes, a murmur started making it way down the line. We heard people saying, "he's quitting." Members of the class were looking behind them to see the unimaginable. William, the class favorite, had competed at the highest level. He could swim fast, run like the wind, and was a beast on the obstacle course. The man was a mentor to the class and a pillar of strength. But at that moment he had finally found something that he couldn't outrun or outperform. The cold water. When he had to sit there and think about the four more days of pain, he broke. He stood up from the water and was walking down the beach towards the bell. He was done.

What happened next surprised me even more. The members of the class who had allowed the demon inside to have a voice started breaking. One by one, guys stood up and walked toward the bell. It was clear that they had been looking for a reason to quit themselves and William had provided it. They figured if he couldn't do it then they couldn't do it either. They had their excuse, and they lined up in droves behind him. I don't remember exactly how many people quit in the next 10 minutes or so, but it was a lot.

I will always be proud of what I felt next. While some had found a personal weakness at the moment, I felt something very different. I felt a power rise from within me. I felt an intense pride. The demon in my mind cowered away while I repeated over and over, "I'm still here" in my mind. I drew strength. I was confident. I was proud, and my determination soured to new heights.

The next few days are a blur. It's hard to remember everything, but I'll never forget what happened that Friday afternoon. They lined us up as they had before. They marched us into the water. I was ready to hit my back and feel the cold of the water again. I felt the pain of the salt into my open wounds. I was ready, but it never came. Instead, the instructor said, "about face." We turned around and saw on top of the sand berm a large American flag. Our loved ones were standing on top under the flag. "Hell Week is secured," the instructor said with a smile. We had made it, and I was thankful. It was my first taste of what it meant to be elite, and I was addicted.

The Smurf Crew was not known for being strong performers physically compared to our larger counterparts. What we had been able to accomplish was to add levity to the situation and to control our minds. The worse it got, the funnier it became. There was no room for negativity because we were finding ways to be positive. We were actively controlling our mental environment, regardless of our external pressures.

Protect Your Mental Hard Drive

Think about the music that we listen to, the movies we watch, and the news feed that we are constantly streaming into our brains throughout the day. There is an onslaught of negative emotion and sentiment laying siege on our minds, even though our lives are entirely separate from the information. I saw a news report once of a man wearing a Santa hat shooting people in Turkey. It made me sick to my stomach and put me in a bad mood for a bit. I can't help but think about how nothing in my life would have changed regardless of whether or not I heard that news. The temperature would have been the same. My kids would have been the same, my wife, money, time, job . . . The list goes on. The only thing that changed was *me*, after allowing the information into my head.

I am in no way saying that ignorance is something to aspire to. Please don't put your head in the sand. But at least allow yourself to look up at the stars. Being aware of our current global and political environments is perfectly healthy and necessary, but allowing those things to ruin your day is wrong. There is no such thing as a bad day, just bad moments. If you let these moments affect an entire day, then you are not doing your job. You are not guarding your mind.

I would urge everyone to be conscious of what you are allowing into your mind. Spend your time thinking about the more beautiful things in life. Spend time in reflection so that you can be more thankful and less hateful. Today is a new day after all, and it is yours to live. There is no news on TV that can make that statement less accurate.

When we allow information into our brains that is not constructive, it is like downloading a virus onto your computer hard drive. It's going to be there a while, and it will affect your performance. You can keep your hard drive clean by using a firewall. Private networks use firewalls to filter information from the internet and onto your private network and computer system. We must do the same with regard to our mind's hard drive. Protect it from negativity and embrace the positive thoughts that will help it run at optimal speeds and produce optimal results.

Do not choose ignorance but be proactive in controlling your thoughts, which will become your beliefs, and which will turn into actions and eventually, your habits. If you allow negative, harmful, and self-defeatist thoughts, then you should expect your efforts to mirror those thoughts closely. The same is true for positive, self-affirming, optimistic thoughts. Elite people know how to filter the information that leads to thoughts. Elite thoughts will lead to elite beliefs, resulting in elite actions and ultimately, elite habits.

Localize Your Data

One way to do this is by localizing the data that you allow into your mind. Remember earlier when we were discussing how you can divide information into two categories – things that you can change, and things that you cannot? If there is an issue in my neighborhood, then I want to know about it. I want to be aware of it because it could affect my family and me. I also want to be mindful because there may be something that I can do about it. It is a problem that is within my sphere of influence. If I choose to keep myself from that information, I am doing the people in my life a disservice by hiding from it.

The further you get from your daily operations, the less impact you will have on the issue. If you live in a big city, then there may be some benefit to knowing what part of town has the most crime. If you watch those crimes on TV every night, however, you are being bombarded by information that you can't use to better your life.

If you apply this to the political, cultural, and economic issues of your country, then you can affect change due to your right to vote. The ability to be a knowledgeable voter is a privilege. Again, this is because it affects you directly and you have a vote that can effect change. The problem is that if you immerse yourself in the 24-hour news cycle constantly, you will see negative results. Whatever your views are, there is a news source for that to tell you how right you are and how wrong everyone else is. The money pumping through those sources has a motive. Lately, the motivation is to make you angry and hateful against ideas that they do not support. The result is harmful to your internal environment. There is nowhere to place that hate. It lives on your hard drive like a virus. It is your responsibility as a voter to be aware of the world around you, but it is also your responsibility as a human being to not allow the sources of that information to make you hateful and miserable.

This same thinking can apply to social media as well. It is hard to keep negative posts from coming across your feed. You will never be asked the question when you log on, "Do you want to see dead bodies and depressing information at lunch today?" Instead, those images and infuriating messages will wander on your feed and into your mind. The only real control that you have is the block button. If there is nothing that you can do to effect change, then there is no room for that kind of negativity in your life. Do not allow other people or interests to implant negativity in your life. Elite people are proactive about surrounding themselves with actionable information.

When you do feel depressing, hateful, or negative thoughts, combat those thoughts with the mental toughness tactics we discussed earlier. Replace those unhelpful thoughts that could quickly lead to actions with positive, helpful, and loving thoughts, and act on those instead. Use self-talk to remind yourself how lucky you are to have what you have. Elite people know how to keep themselves in their optimal state. They know how to regulate emotion and guard their minds against data that is not useful.

Quite simply, elite people know how to take unnecessary distraction out of their backpack and leave them on the ground. When I was in Hell Week, I was excited and felt blessed. I was able to complete what is widely considered the hardest military training in the world because I wasn't weighed down by the negative opinions of the people who didn't believe in me before I left for training. Had I allowed that virus into my mind, I surely would have felt the effects. William, on the other hand, was carrying weight in his backpack and it proved too heavy to bear. He was unable to control his internal environment and failed to make his dream of becoming a Navy SEAL a reality.

For you to get to the elite level, you will need to gain a lot of experience and knowledge. You will also need to place filters in your life that will protect your mental hard drive from viruses that could grow, slow you down, and keep you from realizing your potential. If you can do this, you will be able to develop into the best possible version of yourself. You will begin to enjoy your thoughts and your time with yourself. Your positive outlook will overflow onto the people around you. You will be more productive, have more energy, and be able to let that energy flow into positive directions. If you guard your mind, it will lead to better habits and optimal results.

Becoming Elite!

1. Your brain is a hard drive. Be proactive about what information you allow it to download.
2. Divide information into two categories: What you can control and what you cannot. Fully embrace the things that you can control and learn to let go of the things you cannot.
3. Do not allow external sources of information to become a distraction. If someone around you quits, filter that into productive action. If you are getting constant negativity from a source, then cut that source out of your life. When life starts feeling as though you are lying down in cold water and suffering, focus on being thankful instead of complaining.
4. You are responsible for your thoughts, because they will become actions. Control your thoughts, and you will produce elite actions.

Whatever It Takes

On your path to becoming elite, there will be no substitute for your ability to grind, push past critics, and create the reality that you desire. The structures that we have discussed in this book will help you get there, but they are not some magic pill that can compensate for grit, and the unrelenting desire to succeed. You can bring your vision to reality if you are strong, work hard, and refuse to lose. You have to be willing to do whatever it takes if you intend to become elite.

Taking Command of My Life

Most of this book is about the elements of our life that are within our ability to manage, as is the rest of this story. The sad truth, however, is that there are so many parts of our lives that we never get to choose. We don't decide what family we are born into, how much natural talent lies deep within our DNA, or how much hair we will carry on our heads into our 40s. However, we can choose how well we treat our families. We can determine what we will do with the talent that we were provided, and we can choose how our smile will brighten the day of a stranger, despite the receding hairline.

When something happens to you, outside of your control, you need to make the best of it. You will look back someday and remember your mindset and actions. This memory will make you feel one of two emotions: pride or shame. Create a life that will make you proud. Choose to be a warrior, not a victim.

For a decade I had to live with the needs of the Navy. I did my very best at anything that was in front of me because

I wanted to succeed. Sometimes this means waiting for our vision, especially if our circumstance is outside our ability to control. The question is then, what can we do when finding ourselves unsatisfied? What do we do when we know that we are destined for more but find that circumstance is in our way? When that is the case, we have to take charge and change our situation.

For me, that moment came after having my first child. Looking into my beautiful baby girl's brown eyes changed me. I knew that I wanted to be there for her to experience the birthdays, the growing pains, and the excitement of the younger years. I also knew that if I stayed in the military, I would miss more of these moments than I could bear. The demands of training constantly and deploying meant that a majority of the year, I would be away from home.

I was getting close to the decision point because my enlistment contract was about to expire. As the date got closer, I developed a plan that would allow me to prepare for the future while not leaving my service to the country entirely. The plan involved separating from the Navy to start deploying to combat zones as an independent contractor.

Furthermore, I wanted to prepare for my future and eventually start a new chapter in my life. For that reason, I applied to business school at the University of San Diego. I had always known that I would not be an operator forever and was looking forward to seeing what I could accomplish in a different context. I knew that getting exposure to business would help with that and was excited to get started. The program that I entered is the Master of Science in Global Leadership, and they were very accommodating with my schedule, allowing me to accomplish a great deal of the workload from overseas.

For the first time in my professional life, I was writing my own orders. I was in command and making my own decisions. The result was a high-paying contract with an elite unit, an acceptance letter from a prestigious graduate school program, and most importantly, much more time home with the family. I was still serving my country, spending more time with the people I loved and preparing for the next stage of life. I was rolling, but I was about to realize exactly what I was rolling into.

A Very Long Day

With my new job I worked through the first part of business school and my first deployment with no issues. My second deployment, however, was a very different story. It was summertime, and we had been very busy. My good friend, who I'll call Charles, and I had been involved in high-risk movements every day that week. The result of the intense workload was that my business-school paper's due date was just one day away. I knew that it was time to commit to my school priorities so I cleared my schedule for the following day so that I could spend the day writing and submit the paper before the deadline. Work ran late that night, so I went straight to my room, and I placed my weapon and body armor next to my bed and fell asleep while watching old episodes of *Seinfeld*.

The next morning I woke up to an explosion loud enough to shake the walls. I immediately recognized it as a vehicle-borne improvised explosive device (VBIED), which were common in the area, but this was much closer than usual. I shot up from my bed and put my body armor on, grabbed my gun and ran out my bedroom door. Small arms fire began ringing through the air, and I realized that we were under attack.

As I opened my door I saw a friend of mine with pants on but no shoes and no shirt under his body armor running to the balcony and yelling at our indigenous forces, who were on shift and at the ready, to get over to our front gate, not 50 meters away.

I told him that we needed to get to the roof, and quickly. We both ran to our storage room to grab our helmets and were met by three other operators. I spoke in a Scottish accent while making my *Braveheart* joke that I told you all about earlier (*That'll wake you up in the morning, boys*) and we went to the roof.

What followed was an hour-and-a-half gunfight. The fog of war is real and recalling some of the events is hazy. I remember watching as the wall between the attackers and us slowly provided information about the attacker's location. I watched a series of explosions, my lungs surging, as one after another, they followed the wall to our front door. Our indigenous forces who had been working the front gate were overrun, and some of our operators were taking cover behind the wall in front of me. The enemy was wearing explosive vests and setting themselves off one at a time to blow down our front door. If they were successful, many of the people I was there to protect would die. It was clear that the enemy had no expectation of surviving the day and that we were in for a hell of a fight.

Our makeshift medical facility was directly below my rooftop position, so I had a front row seat when a vehicle carrying three dead bodies drove from the wall to my position. I could tell that they were our indigenous allies who had been guarding the front gate. Right behind that vehicle came another that was carrying a couple of people who were still alive and screaming in pain. I recognized them as the men we had just ordered to run toward the threat moments after the attack had started.

I heard on the radio that Charles, my best friend there, was in the thick of it and was being told to pull back. Those words made my blood burn hot. My hands began trembling with rage as I asked for a couple of guys to move with me to his location to support him. There was some concern that if we left our current position that it would leave us vulnerable for a follow-up attack. I pushed back against the leadership and said that we should send over a fire team to address the immediate threat. The second request worked, and a few of us moved toward Charles's position.

He and the other element were only about 50 meters away, but we had to move tactically because the enemy was inside our defenses. When we had cleared through the compound to the wall, Charles came around the corner and told me that he had just been shot. He said it with the biggest smile that I've ever seen him wear and a hearty, bellowing laugh. I'll admit, it was funny. We both laughed, and I actually thought he was joking at first. I saw the place where the bullet impacted and realized he was serious. It was on his chest and had impacted his body armor. He was lucky. After checking him for wounds, we moved on.

Shortly after, we got the majority of the group together, suppressed the threat, and punched out to the front gate. The gate was damaged, so we left a group there and went back inside to clear the space. Then we cleared it again. It was a long day. It wasn't until later that afternoon that I remembered about my business-school paper that was due any minute.

I went back to my room, got on my computer, and sent an email to my professor. Due to the nature of my work, I couldn't say what was happening, where I was, or why it was important. My concern was that he would think that I had procrastinated, but he did know that I was on a deployment. My email said that it had been a bad day and that I needed more time hoping that he would read between the lines. After writing the email, I went back downstairs to link up with my friends.

I walked into the team room door and asked my boss if there was anything that I could do to help in the aftermath. He mentioned one of the injured indigenous forces was still alive. I knew that he was one of the men who I had ordered into the fight and his injuries were severe. He had been shot but was still alive. While my boss was still speaking, Charles walked past the door. He heard that I was being tasked with a follow-up mission, and before even hearing the details he spoke up. He said, "Nick, if you're going, then put me on it, too." Now that is loyalty. Even after being in a fight all day, taking one to the plate, and being tired, he had my back. I feel obligated to tell you that he was not a fellow Navy SEAL. He was an Army Special Forces veteran, and we worked together as much as we could. Yes, there is a lot of rivalry between all of us special operator types, but at the end of the day, we are all brothers.

The new mission was for a couple of other operators and me to get our seemingly mortally wounded ally to a helicopter (helo) that could fly him to a hospital where he could have surgery. We did not have a place for a helo to land close by, so we had to go into bad-guy country, lock down a field, and wait for the pickup. We chose a spot, loaded up, and took off. The day had started with explosions at six in the morning, and now the sun was already going down. We waited for a while, expecting the helo to get there quickly but got a call saying that they had been delayed and couldn't provide us with an estimated time of arrival (ETA). Keep in mind that we were in a war zone and people were busy.

We sat, and we waited. The good thing about operators is that the worse things get, the funnier it becomes. The jokes were excellent as was the company. We were exhausted but being out in town after a gunfight in the most dangerous time of year kept us cool. We sat there for hours, making jokes, telling stories, and waiting for an attack. Shortly after the sun rose the next day, we got a call from the helo saying that they were inbound. The man who had been shot survived the night and was safely in the hands of people who could help him. We returned home, and our fire team was given that day off to rest.

I'll never forget walking back into my room, laying down my gun and body armor, drenched in sweat, as I collapsed into my chair. The last time that I had been that worn out was Hell Week. My body had been functioning in high gear, survival mode, for over 30 hours, and I was completely and utterly exhausted.

Just then, as my eyes began to close, I remembered my graduate-school paper. I logged onto my email and read my professor's reply. He said that he understood that I had other responsibilities but that he could only extend the deadline by 24 hours. The email had come in the day before, shortly after I sent him my request. I looked at my watch and realized that I only had four hours until the deadline.

There is a hangover that we are all subject to on the other side of adrenaline. When your body and mind function at their optimal potential, there is a crash waiting for you. I had nearly been killed, people had died, and my friend had been shot in the plate. I'd been engaged for over 30 hours without sleep in the blazing heat of the Middle East, but none of that mattered. I had to sit down and write a paper about how the global business environment was changing due to rapid innovation and globalization.

Pushing through the adrenaline hangover wasn't easy. I fought the urge to close my eyes, but the challenge was bigger than that. I fought the urge to stop caring in general, close my computer, and lie down. I pushed through the temptation and sent a well-written, well-researched paper to my professor on time. I received an A.

Be Unbeatable

I wrote that paper because I was not going to let any external force keep me from getting to where I wanted to be. I wanted excellent grades at school, and I refused to allow the enemy's attack to keep me from that. We all have enemies, though they take different shapes. In my case, it was a physical enemy who wanted to cause me permanent harm. In other cases, it is a coworker who does not want you to succeed or competitors who know they would be better off if you were no longer a factor.

In other cases, it's not a person at all. Your enemy may come in the form of a disability or misplacing your faith in an unhealthy belief. Usually, we find ourselves fighting multiple enemies on multiple fronts. If you want to be elite, you must strive to become Unbeatable. For this to happen, you will need to know how to identify the enemy, how to deal with the enemy, and how to keep your focus on the goal, no matter what.

Identifying the Enemy

One thing you can count on is that external circumstance is going to try and keep you from becoming elite. When you notice these forces standing in your way, you must be able to define them as your enemy. The very definition of an enemy is a person who is actively opposed or hostile to someone or something. Another way of saying it is, a thing that harms or weakens something else. You must correctly identify the things that are actively opposing you – the things that are intentionally damaging you and undermining you.

When I was misled about my orders to SEAL training, I did whatever it took to get around the recruiter and get to where I knew I needed to be. When I got orders to the SDV team, I did the best job that I could and was proud to do so. After getting attacked, I refused to let them rob me of my grades, even after volunteering for a follow-up mission that lasted all night. I never needed anyone's approval for me to get out there and take what I wanted. Sometimes it took more time than others, but I got there eventually every time.

Many times in this book we have discussed the different forms that the enemy can take. It can come in the form of a social media addiction that keeps you from being noticed at work or spending time with the people who love you. It can come from the negativity in your mind, telling you that you will never succeed, that you will never be good enough, and that you will never become elite.

Sometimes the enemy looks like the people in our lives that are standing in our way. They may be doing it on purpose to keep you from getting in their way, or they may be behaving that way inadvertently due to what is in their nature. It doesn't matter. If they are harming you or weakening you, they are standing against your vision and may not be the people who you wish to fight against the enemy with.

Dealing with the Enemy

One of the hardest byproducts of identifying an enemy is the emotional toll that it can take. If it is another person, it can hurt. If it is something inside or a part of you, it can be demoralizing. If it is a deadline, it can be stressful. The way that we deal with our own emotions will have a significant impact on how we deal with the enemy. If you allow those negative emotions to guide you, then you will deal with the enemy in a negative way. The result will be your undoing. Do not make yourself an enemy of theirs. Do not hurt them or take the low road. It just does not work, and it will not work for you. Guard your mind, control your thoughts, and continually improve your situation. After all, you are not a victim; you are a warrior.

Warrior mentality is not about fighting or hurting other people. It is about believing in yourself, your preparation, and your ability to never quit. A warrior will take the high road with his or her enemies. There is no reason for harsh words. Simply remove the enemy from your life. Allow it no place in your lifestyle, your routine, or your contact list. Vote with your feet. Your absence will have more of an effect than any negativity ever could.

If social media is harming you, there is no need to make a post about how you are walking away from it. Don't create a scene, just vote with your feet. Limit your time intentionally. Be disciplined and enjoy the space that you have created in your backpack.

If it is a person harming you, then you can vote with your feet. Do not respond with violence or anger. Instead, be a better person. Remove yourself from the harmful people and begin surrounding yourself with the people who are living their lives in ways that you would like to emulate. You will become like the people you hang around, so make sure that they are the right people.

If it is a competitor, be sure to run your race, not theirs. Do not fall for the trap of comparison. Look for ways to innovate and grow. Sure, keep your eyes on the competitor and be aware of what they are doing, but do not let their actions affect your direction. Do not be clouded by emotion. Instead, be happy that you can create something of your own. Be kind to your competitors, even when they do not pay you the same respect. If you decide to play in the mud, you will get dirty. Instead, take the high road. It is the road of the elite.

Focus on the Goal, No Matter What

When dealing with other people, it is essential to be polite and respectful. When addressing your goals, your vision, and your aspirations, you must tap into your primal beast. Remember my resume at the beginning of this book? There were some exceptional headlines, but I let you in on the secret failures in between the lines. Every one of those setbacks was a challenge for both myself and the people around me. I was able to push through because I tapped into the primal state of being that is relentless in the pursuit of excellence.

If someone told me that I could not do something, it only strengthened my resolve. I would look forward to proving the naysayers wrong and drew strength from it. When factors that were outside my ability to control prevented me from getting where I wanted to be, I decided to be patient. I used that time to better prepare, to learn, and to grow. I decided to become the right guy for the job before I had the job. When the opportunity finally presented itself, I rose to the occasion.

The structures and processes within this book will help you a great deal. They will help you become disciplined and systematic in your approach to becoming elite. There is another factor, however. It is the X-factor – the raw, gritty desire to be an unrelenting force. You must fight for what you want. No one will hand it to you. You must be willing to claw your way, tooth and nail, to your success. If you come across a barrier, you can either go around it, climb over it or plow through it. If you experience setbacks, use that extra time as an opportunity to prepare and become a better version of yourself. If you find yourself in deep water, use it as an opportunity to practice mental toughness techniques and stay the course.

You must commit to your plan or you will become a part of someone else's. You will have to stick with it, no matter what gets thrown in your face. You have to want it as much as life itself. The margin between the elite and the status quo is slim. It will take a stable structure in your life, discipline, mental toughness and good people to help you along the way. In the end, the margin is in the X-factor and your relentless pursuit of becoming elite.

What's Next?

We started this process by emptying our backpacks on the ground. We then took note of the things that were keeping us from being able to operate at the elite level, and began exploring what structures we can place in our lives to make us more disciplined in our approach of bringing our vision into reality. We've explored different mental toughness tactics that we can employ to face our internal negative demons and their desire to make us all victims of the game. We then replaced those thoughts with positive thoughts, positive actions, and positive people. We have discussed embracing challenge and disruption in an effort to keep our blades sharp while building mental benchmarks that we can use to achieve our goals. Not bad for a day's work.

What is important to remember is that none of this matters without action. Words vanish and motivation dissipates like a vapor in the air. Action is required. Not tomorrow, we do not know if we will even have a tomorrow. Action matters here and now. What can you do today to improve? As I said before, stop worrying about being right and get excited about being better today than you were yesterday.

You've let go of apathy, laziness, and excuses. After all, life is too short to settle for anything less than being elite.

Acknowledgments

Family

My mom, Susan Hays – I was blessed to have a mother who provided me with an invisible parachute my entire life. She always believed in me but was careful to guide me along the way. Being a mother is hard work and mine always went the extra mile.

My dad, Kirk Hays – I have been blessed with a great father. He showed me that a tough man can have a soft heart, how to work hard at home and on the job, and how to make other people feel valued. I will always look up to him.

My sister, Chelsea Hays – My sister showed me how to dream. She has lived a bright life and will always be a child at heart. She has a knack for seeing the bright side and I hope that it's rubbed off on me.

My wife Ivy and kids Vela, Elijah, and Shiloh – Ivy has always shown love and support, even when I had to spend considerable time away. She has enriched my life and I couldn't ask for another helpmate. Even through the process of creating this book, she has been my guidepost in the same way that Abigail Adams was with our founding father John Adams so many years ago. My children have added another dimension to my life. You are the reason that I want to let my light shine as brightly as possible and why I want to be a positive influence in the lives of others. My family is my "why."

Childhood/Developmental Influence

Moving so much as a kid was hard and I really appreciate everyone out there who welcomed me with open arms, even if my accent was different from yours. While you all mean so much to me, I want to say thank you to my inner circle by location. Utah: Kris Jones, Nick Jones, Kyle Gardner; Arizona: Steve Peyton, Mike Peyton, Chris Greenwalt, Dan Anderson, Roxy Woodward; Mississippi: Joey Katz, Andy Taylor, Clint Degroff, Brian Gordon, Rachel Camburn, Living Stone . . . and about 100 more people; San Diego: Clint Freeman, John Leblanc, Bryan Black, Jesse Garner.

I would not be who I am today if not for you all . . . That's right, I blame you!

Professional Mentors

A large portion of this book is focused on being around the right people. My mentors in this life are such a large part of who I am today that I wanted to thank Daron Cobb for my early development, James Boa for showing me what a team guy looks like, and Jon Gordon for introducing me to a world that I didn't even know existed.

Working in professional sports came at a time in my life when I desperately needed purpose. Thank you to Erik Spoelstra, Dan Quinn, and Thomas Dimitroff for letting me into your lives. I have learned a lot more from you than I ever taught. It's hard to say just how much it means to me but a genuine thank you needs a place in this book.

HBS

My time at Harvard Business School has added another dimension to my approach on life and business. Even more than that, the relationships that I have made there I value dearly. Specifically I want to highlight these individuals: Lisa Hughes, Eugene Soltes, Michael Tushman, Kristian Haigh, John Wilson, Living Group 32, David Mayor, Chase Wise, Jason Wallace, Aaron Kendle, and my great classmates in PLD 25.

Book Process

I want to say a special thank you to my friend, Stanford alum and Harvard classmate Jason Wallace, who helped me considerably in framing the message to drive the best possible product.

Thank you David Mayer for designing the graphics in this book. Being able to work with such a talented friend was an honor and I can't thank you enough.

Book Previews

Telling so much of my life story was an intimidating challenge. To do it well, I wanted to have the rough draft of this book proofread by people who know me well and would provide me accurate feedback and push back when something didn't feel right. My sincerest thanks to Tim Anderson, Jesse Garner, Jon Leblanc, Steven Stien, Jesse Ackerman, Ivy Hays, Patrick Bisher,

Remi Adeleke, Bryan Black, C.C. Chapman, Ian Connole, Mike Peyton, and Joe Murphy.

John Wiley & Sons

Working with Wiley has been a great experience and they have supported me every step of the way. Special thanks to Shannon Vargo and Vicki Adang for helping me with my organization and pushing me in the right directions.

Lost Warriors

To the families of all my brothers who paid the ultimate sacrifice, especially my friends lost during my tenure at SDVT-1. Matt Leathers, Eric Shellenberger, and Brett Marihugh all played significant roles in my life, and losing them affected me deeply. Matt was the first person who took me under his wing when I showed up as a new guy, Shelly was my platoon chief when we lost him, and Brett was the light shining in dark places. Please know that their sacrifices will never be forgotten. I'm not ready to share those stories, but they are my personal definition of what it means to be elite.

About the Author

Nick Hays served his country proudly as a Navy SEAL for 10 years and was awarded the Bronze Star. After leaving the Navy, he worked as a contractor in the Middle East while attending business school at the University of San Diego.

Upon graduating from the Harvard Business Program for Leadership Development, Nick became passionate about helping organizations and teams overcome the problems associated with the need for constant innovation. His focus is on providing teams and leaders with the structure necessary to create cultures that can thrive at the highest level.

His principles have been put to the test by professional and college sports teams, corporations, young presidents organizations, school districts, and nonprofits.

Index